T0017760

NEW YEAR NEW YOU

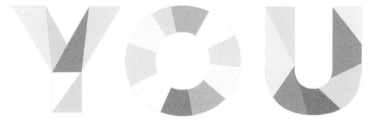

365 BIBLE READINGS

AND PRAYERS

FOR TEENS

WRITTEN BY LAUREN GROVES

B&H
PUBLISHING
NASHVILLE, TENNESSEE

For my little ones, Eden and Ezra.

I pray your bedtime prayer stays on your lips for the rest of your days: "Thank You for loving me. Help me love You."

Copyright © 2022 by B&H Publishing Group
All rights reserved.
Printed in China

978-1-0877-6850-2

Published by B&H Publishing Group
Nashville, Tennessee

Dewey Decimal Classification: J242.2
Subject Heading: DEVOTIONAL LITERATURE / TEENAGERS / CHRISTIAN LIFE

1 2 3 4 5 6 • 26 25 24 23 22

INTRODUCTION

Hey friends! If your life is anything like mine was as a Christian teenager, it's filled with distractions pulling my attention from God: drama with friends, social media, relationships, peer pressure, and a thousand other things. I found it really hard to spend intentional time with God, wondering, *If prayer is the way I talk to God, why don't I want to do it more? Why am I so distracted?*

The good news is, God has given us an amazing tool as we learn how to communicate with Him: the Bible! In this book, you'll find a daily Scripture passage that tells us something about God and His character followed by a short prayer. You may take the whole year to read this book or you may work through it in a matter of months. You may get three pages into the book and then realize a month has gone by without opening it. There's lots of grace. Just turn to the day's date, and keep going.

I pray this little book begins a lifetime of reading what God has spoken in His Word and responding to Him with honesty, praise, and confidence—that it creates a habit of prayer in a world of distractions. I also hope the prayers found in this book are your starting point, but not the final destination. I pray these prayers draw you toward God and His truths for all the days of your life.

With love,
Lauren

JANUARY 1

*I have loved you with an everlasting love;
therefore, I have continued to extend
faithful love to you.*

Dear God, thank You that as this new year begins, I remember Your love is forever! Before I was even born, You knew me and loved me. While I know Your love is perfect, I still look to other things and people for contentment. I try to satisfy myself with possessions—new clothes or technology or games—but I know those things won't last. I fill the empty places in my heart with people's approval, but I know that even the kindest people will let me down. You are the only one who has been completely faithful in the past and will be completely faithful in the future. Help me look to You as the central source of love in my life. Thank You for being with me throughout this year and every year to follow, and for never letting me down.

JANUARY 2

2 TIMOTHY 2:13

If we are faithless, he remains faithful,
for he cannot deny himself.

Jesus, thank You that even when I am having a hard time believing in You, You don't abandon me. There are so many times I doubt You. I wonder if there really is a God, and if there is, how do I know if I am following the right one? I know it's normal to doubt, but God, I wonder if my doubts change the way You feel about me. But they don't. You are faithful! Thank You for reminding me that Your feelings for me never change. Will You give me faith when I doubt You? Help me to trust You even when my heart is unsure. Give me faith when I am faithless.

JANUARY 3

ROMANS 14:19

So then, let us pursue what promotes peace and what builds up one another.

Father in heaven, the Bible tells me it takes commitment and effort to love others with Your love. In a world that says people should constantly fight with one another, it feels weird to work toward peace and build others up. People expect me to be hateful when someone disagrees with me. But You have done so much to show Your love for me! I want to show Your love to others, too. Will You give me a love for others that makes no sense to the rest of the world? Help me seek peace even when I disagree with others. Help me encourage people even when I am being torn down. Thank You, God, for giving me strength to run after peace, even when it doesn't make sense to people around me.

NEW

JANUARY 4

1 Chronicles 16:29

*Ascribe to the LORD the glory of his name; bring
an offering and come before him. Worship the
LORD in the splendor of his holiness.*

God, You are holy! You are set apart from everything in this world. Your Word reminds me there is amazing splendor and beauty in Your holiness. It's so easy to look around and become obsessed with the world's definition of beauty. It tells me I have to be the right size or wear the right clothes—that I have to have the perfect skin and hair or that I should have my own look but not stand out too much. I look for others people's approval by looking in a mirror. But God, that leaves me feeling empty. Will You help me reflect Your beautiful holiness? Give me confidence to stop obsessing over the world's beauty standards and start chasing holiness. Thank You for setting me apart and for helping me look more and more like You.

JANUARY 5

Romans 8:16–17

The Spirit himself testifies together with our spirit that we are God's children, and if children, also heirs—heirs of God and coheirs with Christ—if indeed we suffer with him so that we may also be glorified with him.

Holy Spirit, by trusting in Jesus, You help me experience joy! Thank You so much. I sometimes doubt that truth. Different lies whisper in my head. Some say following Jesus will suffocate me and I won't be truly free unless I walk away. Other times, they ask if I should depend on Jesus. If I do, the lies whisper, *I won't be able to ever do what I want.* If I'm being honest, I'm sometimes tempted to believe those lies. But I know what You have for me is far greater than anything I could ever want for myself. I am a child of God! Because my trust is in Christ, I can experience joy now and for eternity. Help me remember those truths when I am tempted to put my hope in anything other than Jesus. I love You.

JANUARY 6

LUKE 7:6

Jesus went with them, and when he was not far from the house, the centurion sent friends to tell him, "Lord, don't trouble yourself, since I am not worthy to have you come under my roof."

Lord, the Bible tells me all have sinned. No one is worthy of Your love. I know this is true of everyone, but when I am with other Christians, I sometimes feel like the worst sinner—the most unworthy to be around You. But Jesus, You came to earth. You chose to be with us. I know I'm unworthy of Your love, but You made it possible for me to come to You freely, even when I feel like the worst sinner in the room. Help me come to You in full confidence—without being ashamed. Thank You for choosing me and for making me confident in Your love.

JANUARY 7

JEREMIAH 17:7–8

The person who trusts in the LORD, whose confidence indeed is the LORD, is blessed. He will be like a tree planted by water: it sends its roots out toward a stream, it doesn't fear when heat comes, and its foliage remains green. It will not worry in a year of drought or cease producing fruit.

Dear God, I know I can trust You when I am afraid. As long as I am living in this world, I know fear will come. Because of sin, there is so much to be afraid of—death, disease, or losing the people I love most. But Lord, You can be trusted even if I face all those things. I can run to You when fear suffocates me. Please remind me that when I draw close to You, I can grow into a stronger Christian—like a tree planted by water. I want to be rooted in You, trusting You in every circumstance, no matter what comes. Thank You so much for giving me the opportunity to come close to You in my fear.

JANUARY 8

JOHN 17:17

*Sanctify them by the truth;
your word is truth.*

Father, arguing and disagreements are all around me. Everyone tells me I have to take a stand on every single topic. If I don't, I am weak and unstable. But You tell me that when arguments surround me, I can focus on truth: Your truth. Will You help me stand firm on Your Word when I am unsure about an issue? Will You give me confidence to trust You for answers when I simply don't know? Thank You for being the one who holds all truth and for giving me a sure place to stand.

COLOSSIANS 1:9–10

We are asking that you may be filled with the knowledge of his will in all wisdom and spiritual understanding, so that you may walk worthy of the Lord, fully pleasing to him: bearing fruit in every good work and growing in the knowledge of God.

God, it seems like there are a thousand things I need to do in a day. The pressure is so heavy! I want to do it all, and I want to be the best at everything I try. I don't want my weaknesses to ever show. But Your Word says the one who is weak can become strong by Your power. When I try to be strong in my own power, no matter how hard I try, I can't walk in Your ways. Help me grow in Your strength instead of relying on mine. I want to grow so much in You that everyone around me sees You through me. Thank You for being my reliable strength. You are truly the best at everything. I love You, Lord.

JANUARY 10

PSALM 143:1

LORD, hear my prayer. In your faithfulness listen to my plea, and in your righteousness answer me.

Jesus, I confess I feel like a burden to You. How could such a great God—the God who created the whole earth—care so deeply about me and my worries? I feel ashamed about the things that make me anxious. But Your Word tells me You want me to cry out to You when I am worried or anxious. You tell me to not feel hesitant around You. You are gentle with me when I pray, and You listen to me when I ask for answers. Because of Your kindness, I know I can trust You with the big things and the small things. Will You give me strength and willingness to come to You when I feel anxious? Thank You for hearing my prayers and listening to my cries.

JANUARY 11

Genesis 28:15

"Look, I am with you and will watch over you wherever you go. I will bring you back to this land, for I will not leave you until I have done what I have promised you."

Dear Lord, change is hard. Friends move away. College is approaching. Breakups happen. I sometimes worry I will have to leave everything I know for a reason I can't control. But even if I leave what is familiar, You are with me. Even when everything is uncertain, You remain the same. You will always be with me no matter what. Help me put all my trust in You. Thank You, God, for keeping Your promises and for never leaving me.

NEW

JANUARY 12

PSALM 32:7–8

You are my hiding place; you protect me from trouble. You surround me with joyful shouts of deliverance. "I will instruct you and show you the way to go; with my eye on you, I will give counsel."

Father, I know trouble in this world is inevitable. But You promise to protect me. I often struggle to trust You—especially when I am making big decisions like what I will do after high school or how to leave an unhealthy friendship. I feel like I have to weigh all my options, and if I make one wrong choice, it will affect my whole life. But God, even if my choices lead to something hard, You will be with me. Will You help me trust You for protection, and will You give me joy even if things don't go my way? Thank You for surrounding me and for being my hope when I am making decisions. I know I am safe with You no matter what.

JANUARY 13

1 CORINTHIANS 15:57

But thanks be to God, who gives us the victory through our Lord Jesus Christ!

Dear Jesus, thank You for giving me victory over sin! Even when I am fighting temptation and even when I mess up, You provide a way out of my struggles. You walk with me and help me leave the things that hurt You. Satan often tells me You would never save someone like me. But Your Word says that if I place my trust in You, You will save me! I don't have to live in guilt or shame anymore. I can win my fight against temptation. Help me remember that, Lord! Give me a heart that wants to obey You above all else. Thank You for Your victory over sin, and thank You for letting me share in that victory.

JANUARY 14

PROVERBS 20:3

*Honor belongs to the person who ends a dispute,
but any fool can get himself into a quarrel.*

God, because You are a God of peace, You help me end arguments. It is my nature to argue with people, to constantly prove to everyone else that I am right. If I am not careful, I'm the one who starts arguments. I pick fights to show off how smart I am. God, those actions aren't from You. You want me to show others what Your peace looks like. Will You help me be a person who ends arguments instead of starting them? Will You give me wisdom to know when to leave conversations that don't honor You? Thank You for being the ultimate example of peace! Help me reflect You in all I say and do.

JANUARY 15

Luke 10:1

*After this, the Lord appointed seventy-two others,
and he sent them ahead of him in pairs to every
town and place where he himself was about to go.*

Dear Lord, thank You for putting other Christians in my life! The world tells me that being myself is the most important thing I could do. It's easy to focus on following You on my own and forget about my Christian community. Your plan was for people to live with and help one another, and the Bible tells me You care about Christians having relationships with each other. Put Your love for Your people inside my heart, Jesus! When I am tempted to only care about myself, remind me of the people You have placed in my life. I want to follow You with other Christians by my side.

NEW

JANUARY 16

MATTHEW 14:19

Then he commanded the crowds to sit down on the grass. He took the five loaves and the two fish, and looking up to heaven, he blessed them. He broke the loaves and gave them to the disciples, and the disciples gave them to the crowds.

God in heaven, You can make so much out of nothing! This Bible verse reminds me that with only a young boy's small lunch, You fed everyone who gathered to hear Your teachings. Lord, I'm a lot like the little boy with a little bit of lunch. I don't have a lot to offer You. I don't make much money, and I don't have a lot of extra time in my life. But I know You make much with only a little. Even though I am just a kid, and even though I cannot give You everything You deserve, will You do big things with what I have? Thank You for using everything I offer You for good.

JANUARY 17

EPHESIANS 6:13

For this reason take up the full armor of God, so that you may be able to resist in the evil day, and having prepared everything, to take your stand.

Lord, saying "no" to sin is such a battle. My heart wants to take part in sin all the time. Some of my friends are having sex or drinking, and it's so easy to convince myself those things aren't that big of a deal. I can make a little exception, just this once. But one exception turns into a full-on war before I know it. It's tiring, God. I find myself wanting to just give up and let sin win. Will you help me look to Your Word as I fight sin? You promise that through Jesus, You are all the armor I need. I can stand firm in truth, righteousness, peace, faith, and my salvation. I am so grateful that You help me resist sin and fight every temptation I face.

JANUARY 18

ROMANS 12:2

Do not be conformed to this age, but be transformed by the renewing of your mind, so that you may discern what is the good, pleasing, and perfect will of God.

Father God, in a world that tells me to be myself, I know that spending time with You makes me stand out. My friends tell me to follow my heart, but honestly, following my heart almost always leaves me empty and wanting more. Will You direct my heart to You instead? Please inspire me to read Your Word and pray. I want my mind to be more like Yours and less like the world's. That's how I want to stand out. Thank You for teaching me that the best kind of person I can be is one who follows You.

JANUARY 19

JOHN 13:7

Jesus answered him, "What I'm doing you don't realize now, but afterward you will understand."

Jesus, even when I don't understand what You're doing, I can trust You. I get excited about my plans, like what school I want to go to or what job I think I want. But when it looks like things aren't going to go how I planned, I start to doubt You. I feel a little like the disciples who thought they would spend the rest of their lives following You from town to town in Israel. They probably doubted You when You died on the cross. But the whole time, You knew what was best. Will You help me trust that You are the only one who knows what is right? Thank You for knowing and doing the best thing for me every single time, Jesus! If You knew what was best when You died on the cross, You know what is best now, too.

NEW

JANUARY 20

Psalm 22:9–10

It was you who brought me out of the womb, making me secure at my mother's breast. I was given over to you at birth; you have been my God from my mother's womb.

Dear God, You have cared for me all my life. You created me! I trust You won't stop now. I admit I feel anxious about the future. The pressure of growing up and going out on my own is intense. Sometimes I think I have to figure everything out on my own to prove I am responsible. Every single decision feels like it will make or break my future. Help me trust You when my anxiety overwhelms me and when the pressure of growing up feels like too much. You have always provided for me. You won't stop now. Thank You for being trustworthy, God.

JANUARY 21

PROVERBS 12:19

Truthful lips endure forever,
but a lying tongue, only a moment.

Lord God, I am sometimes tempted to lie when I think it will help me. But a lie will never last. Even if I am the only person who knows I lied, You know, too. It's easy to tell people what I think they want to hear, to tell white lies so they will like me and appreciate me. But what good are people's compliments if they aren't true? Your Word tells me truth lasts forever. Help me think about eternity when I am tempted to lie. Give me courage to tell the truth even when it is hard. Thank You, God, for loving me even though You know the truth about me and my sin.

JANUARY 22

PSALM 119:4

You have commanded that your precepts be diligently kept.

God, I want to be someone who brings You joy by obeying Your Word! But how can I obey it if I don't know it? With all of my commitments—school, friends, sports, and family—it is so easy to make reading the Bible the last priority in my life. I always think I will get to it later, but I put it off. Help me make reading and obeying Your Word my top priority! I want to walk in the truths You have laid out for me in the Bible. Thank You for giving me Your Word so I can know how to follow You.

JANUARY 23

PSALM 34:1

I will bless the LORD at all times;
his praise will always be on my lips.

Father in heaven, I want to praise You in everything I say and do. It's easy to believe my actions and words only reflect me. If I do something wrong or right, it only affects me. But what does it say about You when my words are unkind? How am I showing people who You are? I want my words to lead to Your praise alone! I can praise You when I am at school, when I am with my friends, and when I am alone—when I am doing anything at all! I don't always praise You with my words and actions, but I want to. Please show me how. Give me a heart that constantly praises You, God.

NEW

JANUARY 24

JOHN 3:16

For God loved the world in this way: He gave his one and only Son, so that everyone who believes in him will not perish but have eternal life.

Dear Jesus, You are the only one who brings eternal life! Without Your salvation, my life would be defined by my sin. I admit I sometimes wonder if Your sacrifice was enough to save me. I know my heart and all the ways I sin. I know how unloving I can be. On my own, I don't deserve salvation. But when I start to think my sins are too big for Your sacrifice, I am doubting Your love. Will You give me full confidence in Your gift of salvation? Thank You for living, dying, and rising again so that I, and everyone who believes in You, can have eternal life!

JANUARY 25

1 CORINTHIANS 2:9

But as it is written, "What no eye has seen, no ear has heard, and no human heart has conceived—God has prepared these things for those who love him."

God, You are the only one who can satisfy my desires. I confess I spend a lot of time wishing I had what other people have. It seems like someone is always telling me about the next thing I need. Whether it is name-brand clothes, a movie-worthy relationship, or being in that group of friends—if I focus on what I don't have, I feel discontent and wish I had more. God, will You help me look to You when I feel unsatisfied? Thank You for turning my heart toward Your love, and thank You that all my needs and wants will be met in heaven with You.

JANUARY 26

PROVERBS 25:28

*A person who does not control his temper
is like a city whose wall is broken down.*

Father God, thank You for self-control, especially when I am angry. On the days when it feels like nothing goes my way, it is so hard to control my anger. I feel like my emotions are controlling me! I'm so tempted to say or do something that will hurt someone else. It's almost like I want others to feel what I am feeling. But God, when I trust in You, I don't have to be guided by my emotions. I can control my anger when it feels impossible because You are helping me. I want to trust in You for self-control. Give me a heart that seeks to love others instead of hurting them.

JANUARY 27

ROMANS 6:1–2

What should we say then? Should we continue in sin so that grace may multiply? Absolutely not! How can we who died to sin still live in it?

Jesus, thank You for Your grace! Without You, I would be completely controlled by my sinful heart. But Jesus—sometimes it's easy to use Your forgiveness as an excuse to give into sin. I think that because I am forgiven, it would be okay to disobey You. But Your Word says that attitude does not honor You. God, I don't want to take advantage of You! You saved me from the punishment of sin so I can live freely in Your grace. Help me say "no" to sin! Thank You for being kind to me and forgiving me when I sin. Please continue to make my heart more like Yours as I enjoy Your grace.

NEW

JANUARY 28

JOSHUA 1:7

"Above all, be strong and very courageous to observe carefully the whole instruction my servant Moses commanded you. Do not turn from it to the right or the left, so that you will have success wherever you go."

Dear God, I have so many decisions to make. I have to decide what friends to hang out with, what to do after high school, what extra activities will look best on my résumé . . . the list goes on and on. It feels like everyone is watching to see what decisions I will make. It's overwhelming. But Your Word tells me that following You is always the right decision. When there are a thousand choices in front of me, I can focus on You and trust You to show me what to do. Real success comes from following You. Will You help me remember that? Help me fix my eyes on You instead of worrying about what people think of me and my decisions.

JANUARY 29

COLOSSIANS 3:23

Whatever you do, do it from the heart, as something done for the Lord and not for people.

Lord, help me remember that I do not have to work to earn people's love or respect. All the responsibilities I have can sometimes feel like burdens. I want to do them all well, and I want people to praise me for my hard work. Your Word, though, reminds me that I shouldn't seek people's approval. Everything I say and do should be done for You. Jesus, help me focus on You when I am trying to get things done. Give me energy when I feel tired, and excitement for all You are doing in and through me. Thank You for helping me honor You with all the responsibilities You have given me.

JANUARY 30

1 Peter 2:9

But you are a chosen race, a royal priesthood, a holy nation, a people for his possession so that you may proclaim the praises of the one who called you out of darkness into his marvelous light.

God, thank You so much for choosing me to be Your child and making me secure in You! Insecurity rumbles at every corner of my life. Sometimes it scares me—so many things in life aren't guaranteed. From little things like not getting into the same classes with my friends to big things like losing family members, I know nothing is sure, and that terrifies me. I am so thankful that even when things change around me, for good or bad, I can always trust You. You hold my life in Your hands. I can never lose You, God. Your Word says I am Yours.

JANUARY 31

LUKE 11:54

They were lying in wait for him to trap him in something he said.

King Jesus, people tried to catch You in sin the whole time You lived on earth, but they never could. You never sinned! I can't imagine going even one day without sinning, much less a whole life. When I'm tempted to sin, I usually give in. Sometimes I don't even realize I am disobeying You! When I face temptation, remind me how You were tempted over and over again and never gave in. Help me follow You and choose Your way even when sin tries to trap me. I want to live like You, Jesus!

FEBRUARY 1

GENESIS 1:26

Then God said, "Let us make man in our image, according to our likeness. They will rule the fish of the sea, the birds of the sky, the livestock, the whole earth, and the creatures that crawl on the earth."

God, I love the things You created! I am so thankful I can enjoy them. It's easy to go about my life without appreciating all Your creative work. Nature feels normal, but when I stop and really think about it, anything that lives is a miracle! You created all these things—land, trees, animals—from absolutely nothing. Make me someone who appreciates Your creation so that when I see what You've made, I worship You.

FEBRUARY 2

1 JOHN 1:9

If we confess our sins, he is faithful and righteous to forgive us our sins and to cleanse us from all unrighteousness.

Jesus, I praise You. When You saved me from my sin, You made me pure. You forgave me and cleansed me of my sin! I don't always live like I have been forgiven, though. I still sin. When I choose my way instead of Yours, I feel ashamed and wonder if I messed up too badly for You to forgive me. Your Word says I can never clean my life up enough to be worthy of Your forgiveness. Only You are worthy of God's favor. Give me confidence in Your power to forgive, and help me share that power with everyone I know. Thank You for being faithful and just to clean my heart from sin, Jesus.

FEBRUARY 3

JOHN 6:63

The Spirit is the one who gives life. The flesh doesn't help at all. The words that I have spoken to you are spirit and are life.

Holy Spirit, I want to listen to Your voice instead of my sinful mind. My mind tells me I am not good enough. When I look at Instagram or watch videos, I see the body I should have, the clothes I should be wearing, the popularity I should chase after. I sometimes want those things so bad that when I don't have them, I become bitter. I need Your help, Holy Spirit! When my mind tells me I'm not good enough, remind me that life from Jesus is all I need! Thank You for speaking to me!

FEBRUARY 4

1 CORINTHIANS 3:7

So, then, neither the one who plants nor the one who waters is anything, but only God who gives the growth.

Father God, thank You for using me in Your plan to save people. There are people all around me who don't trust You as the one and only God—my friends, my family, my classmates. It's scary to share Your good news with people who don't know anything about You. What if I offend them? What if I say something wrong? I don't want to be the reason they never believe. God, help me remember You are the one who causes spiritual growth. I don't have to be scared about messing anything up. You are in control! I just need to be obedient to share the gospel. Give me courage to share Your good news, and when I do, let those who hear believe in You.

FEBRUARY 5

MATTHEW 6:14–15

*For if you forgive others their offenses,
your heavenly Father will forgive you as well.
But if you don't forgive others, your Father
will not forgive your offenses.*

Dear God, I need Your help to forgive others like You forgive me. Some friends I trusted let me down. I feel betrayed, misunderstood, and hurt. But when I think about my life, I realize I have hurt You even more than my friends have hurt me. Every time I choose sin, I let You down. And yet You still forgive me! I want to extend that same forgiveness to people. Help me remember that, and help me to forgive others as You forgive me. Thank You for not holding my sin against me, heavenly Father. I love You.

FEBRUARY 6

MARK 10:45

For even the Son of Man did not come to be served, but to serve, and to give his life as a ransom for many.

Dear Jesus, thank You for coming to this earth to serve me! I am not like You. I am a sinner. I often think of myself before considering anyone else. I know this is wrong. The world tells me I should love and serve myself before anyone else. I am tempted to be inconsiderate and unkind by putting my wants above others. But You—the God of the universe who deserves everything—gave Your life for people like me. I want to serve You in return. Thank You for serving me with Your life. Will You give me a generous heart so I can serve You with my life, too?

FEBRUARY 7

DEUTERONOMY 12:7

*You will eat there in the presence of
the LORD your God and rejoice with your
household in everything you do, because
the LORD your God has blessed you.*

Father God, I want to be a better celebrater of You as the giver of every good gift. But it's so easy to celebrate things I can see, touch, and feel without once thinking of You. I celebrate good grades, I celebrate my birthday, I celebrate little and big achievements. Even though I know You give me all these things, I don't always remember to thank You. Please help me to remember You in all my earthly wins. I want to celebrate Your goodness more than anything else in my life! Thank You for all Your gifts, Father.

FEBRUARY 8

ROMANS 11:33

Oh, the depth of the riches and the wisdom and the knowledge of God! How unsearchable his judgments and untraceable his ways!

God, Your wisdom and knowledge are endless! Sometimes I forget how amazing that is. With a touch of a button, I can find out almost anything. But a computer knows only a fragment of what You know. You know everything that has happened in public and behind closed doors. You know the truth behind every scientific theory. Your mind holds all the things I wish I could search the Internet for. I know I can trust You to always do what is best for me. God, please give me wisdom. Help me trust You as the source of all knowledge. Thank You that Your knowledge and wisdom go deeper and wider than I can imagine!

FEBRUARY 9

NEHEMIAH 8:10

*"Do not grieve, because the joy of
the LORD Is your strength."*

Gracious God, because of You, I can choose joy
on the hardest days of my life. Sometimes when I
am sad, I feel hopeless and completely alone, like
no one in the world understands what I am going
through. But You know me inside and out, God.
Despite all my sadness and grief, You promise You
will make me strong with joy. Help my happiness
and hope to come from You, not what happens
around me. Give me hope in my sadness. Thank You
for always being there for me, for never letting me
go through anything alone, and for giving me joy!

FEBRUARY 10

ROMANS 7:14–15

For we know that the law is spiritual, but I am of the flesh, sold as a slave under sin. For I do not understand what I am doing, because I do not practice what I want to do, but I do what I hate.

Lord, Your Word tells me You want me to break my sin patterns. It's hard to obey when disobedience comes so naturally, especially when I see people doing the same thing without getting into any trouble. Before I know it, I am disobeying You, too. But Your Spirit helps me free myself from sin! It's not by my own ability, but by Your power. You give me the strength to overcome sins like lying, gossiping, worshiping things besides You—the list goes on and on. Help me stop living in sin. Thank You for never giving up on me.

FEBRUARY 11

EXODUS 20:3–4

Do not have other gods besides me. Do not make an idol for yourself, whether in the shape of anything in the heavens above or on the earth below or in the waters under the earth.

Father, I set my heart on things other than You all the time. I prioritize extra sleep over reading my Bible, getting ready in the morning over praying to You, texting the person I like instead of paying attention at church, and looking at my phone for advice instead of listening for Your voice. When these things get in the way of my relationship with You, they become my enemies. Help me put everything that takes my attention away from You in its place. Give me a love for You that overwhelms every other thing I love. Thank You, God, for being patient with me and calling me back to You. Nothing is more important than You.

FEBRUARY 12

DEUTERONOMY 6:6–7

These words that I am giving you today are to be in your heart. Repeat them to your children. Talk about them when you sit in your house and when you walk along the road, when you lie down and when you get up.

God, it's easy to believe the Bible is boring, that it doesn't apply to my life today. I sometimes feel like I am wasting my time reading it, especially when I don't understand what I am reading. But I know I'm not wasting time. Your Word gives life! Your Word applies to every area of my life. Help me love Your Word, and help me when it doesn't feel relevant to my life. I want to remember what You have said and how it applies when I am with my friends, when I am taking tests, and when I am playing sports or just having fun. Give me a mind that loves and remembers Your Word, and a heart that treasures what You say. Thank You for giving me Your Word, the Bible.

FEBRUARY 13

REVELATION 21:5

Then the one seated on the throne said,
"Look, I am making everything new."

God of heaven, You see everything, and one day, You will fix everything that's wrong in the world. But I sometimes wonder if You know what's really going on. When I look at this world, I see so much hurt and pain everywhere. From bullies at school to people going hungry—it seems like something is wrong every day and everywhere. It breaks my heart, God. But Your Word says You see all of it—every bit of good and every bit of bad—and if it breaks my heart, it breaks Yours a thousand times more. Thank You for seeing everything, and thank You for being the one who will make all things right one day soon.

FEBRUARY 14

GENESIS 2:18

Then the LORD God said, "It is not good for the man to be alone. I will make a helper corresponding to him."

God, thank You for creating people to need one another. It's easy to believe my relationships don't matter as long as I am following You. I find myself wanting to spend time alone or being annoyed at having to spend time with others. It's just easier to focus on myself, to spend time with my phone or a book or the TV rather than with people. I know it's okay to be alone sometimes, but You created people for one another. I don't want to miss out on the good gift of community. Your Word reminds me that my relationships are important to You. Help me to prioritize them. Thank You for the people You have placed in my life.

FEBRUARY 15

JAMES 4:6

But he gives greater grace.
Therefore he says: God resists the proud
but gives grace to the humble.

Father, how do You always have more grace to give? Even after trusting in You, I have done some terrible things. I have done and thought things that not even my parents or friends know about. Yet You know everything, God—everything—and You still love me! I sometimes doubt You could love someone like me, but I know that's a lie. You promise to give more grace whether I do something that feels small, like telling a white lie, or huge—like sneaking into a party with drugs and drinking. Will You help me grow in that grace? Will You make me look more like Jesus? I want to say "no" to every temptation, big and small. Thank You for the grace You have given me so far and the grace You will give me in the future.

FEBRUARY 16

ISAIAH 43:1

"Do not fear, for I have redeemed you; I have called you by your name; you are mine."

Father, sometimes I am afraid You will take Your love away from me. When I lie to my parents or gossip about a friend, I feel like I let You down. How could You still love me when I knowingly sin? But Your Word reminds me how You chose me to be Your child. I am secure in You. You know me, You know all my sins, and You still made me Yours. Thank You for calling me, God! Give me confidence that You'll never leave me because I am Yours.

FEBRUARY 17

MATTHEW 6:26

"Consider the birds of the sky: They don't sow or reap or gather into barns, yet your heavenly Father feeds them. Aren't you worth more than they?"

God, thank You for giving me everything I need. When I think about the future, I have a lot of questions. Will I make the grades I need to make? Will I let my family down if I don't get in to the right college? What if no one wants to date me? My mind spins with all the questions, and eventually, I just freeze. Help me remember You hold my future in Your hands, God. You will always give me what I need, even if it doesn't look like what I want. Thank You for being trustworthy.

FEBRUARY 18

JOHN 14:19

In a little while the world will no longer see me, but you will see me. Because I live, you will live too.

Jesus, because You died on the cross and rose again, I get to live in eternity with You. But Jesus, it's so easy to believe the lies I hear in my head: *God wouldn't actually save someone like me; I will never be able to stop sinning; my disobedience defines me; God will never accept me.* When I try to quiet those voices on my own, I can't. They're too loud. I need You to help me. Help me listen to Your voice instead of lies. Give me ears to hear You, Lord. Thank You for quieting the voices in my mind and reminding me that sin doesn't define my life anymore—You do!

FEBRUARY 19

EPHESIANS 6:10

*Finally, be strengthened by the Lord
and by his vast strength.*

God, I am full of pride, always thinking of myself. The world tells me that if I believe in myself, I can do anything. But when I spend all my time trying to prove myself to the world, I fail. Even when I get what I thought I wanted, it leaves me empty and wanting more. But You didn't say I could do anything I set my mind on. You tell me it's only by Your strength that I have any power. Give me humility, God. Help me remember that all of my accomplishments are through Your power. Thank You for giving me the grace and humility to rely on You instead of me.

FEBRUARY 20

JAMES 4:14

*Yet you do not know what tomorrow will bring—
what your life will be! For you are like vapor that
appears for a little while, then vanishes.*

King Jesus, I praise You because I don't have to worry about tomorrow! You are already there, and You are in control. Still, I spend so much time worrying about the future. I imagine all kinds of worst-case scenarios. When I do that, I don't get to enjoy Your good gifts; I am too afraid I will lose them. My worry keeps me from experiencing joy, hope, and happiness, and I end up sad and scared. Jesus, remind me that You are in control of all things, including my future. No matter what my future looks like, even if my worst-case scenarios do come true, You are there. You provide me with everything I need. Thank You for giving me hope even when I'm worried and scared.

FEBRUARY 21

GENESIS 3:1

*Now the serpent was the most cunning of all
the wild animals that the LORD God had made.
He said to the woman, "Did God really say,
'You can't eat from any tree in the garden'?"*

Father God, I know that any time I doubt You, it's not a coincidence. Satan wants me to question Your goodness. When Satan tempted Eve in the garden, he convinced her to doubt You really wanted her best. I sometimes wonder that, too, God. Do You have my best at heart? I listen to the voice that says I should choose my way because I am the only one who knows what is best for my life. I want to respond to that voice with confidence. I want to believe, with everything in me, that Your way is always best—and it is! I don't ever have to mistrust You. You are good. You always want what is best for me. Thank You for helping me trust You, even when I am tempted to question Your goodness.

FEBRUARY 22

PROVERBS 10:18

*The one who conceals hatred has lying lips,
and whoever spreads slander is a fool.*

Lord, Your Word makes it clear I shouldn't bad-mouth anyone. But it's so easy to give into the temptation to talk behind people's backs! Almost everyone I know accepts it as normal. It's easy to forget how much You hate it. When someone wants to talk about another person with me, will You give me the strength to leave that conversation? I want to treat other people as I want to be treated, and that includes only speaking what is true, good, and kind. Thank You for always speaking truth in love. Help me do the same for others.

FEBRUARY 23

PSALM 139:14

I will praise you because I have been remarkably and wondrously made. Your works are wondrous, and I know this very well.

Dear God, thank You. When You created me, You gave me worth. I have to admit I feel unworthy a lot of the time, especially when I compare myself to others. Sometimes it is what I look like, sometimes it's that I want to be dating someone, and sometimes it's even how much faith I have. There will always be an area where I don't think I measure up. But my worth doesn't come from any of those things. I have worth because You created me. How remarkable that is! Help me remember my worth when I am tempted to compare myself to others. Thank You for creating me and placing value on my life.

FEBRUARY 24

EXODUS 14:14

*The LORD will fight for you,
and you must be quiet.*

Father God, sometimes I forget I don't have to argue with others, because You fight for me. I admit this is a struggle. I always think I have to stand up for myself. Because You are a strong God, I should be strong like You. I get defensive when people question what I believe. But I don't have to be strong, because You are strong already. You say to be humble and kind. Help me to choose humility over defensiveness and kindness over arguments. Thank You for fighting for me in ways I can't even see.

NEW

FEBRUARY 25

REVELATION 3:20

*See! I stand at the door and knock. If anyone
hears my voice and opens the door, I will come
in to him and eat with him, and he with me.*

Jesus, I sometimes think there is a formula for success. If I make all the right choices and work hard
enough, I will have everything I dream of. But I know
You tell Your children to live by a different formula.
You ask me to set aside my plans to follow You—
even when it doesn't make sense to the rest of the
world and even when it might not look like "success." I want to joyfully say "yes" to anything You ask
of me, Jesus! Will You give me courage to always
say "yes" to You? Thank You for Your amazing plan,
and for inviting me to be a part of it.

FEBRUARY 26

DEUTERONOMY 33:27

The God of old is your dwelling place, and underneath are the everlasting arms.

Heavenly Father, when my life is chaotic, You are my safe place of rest. So much overwhelms me. Between school, friends, activities, and chores, I am convinced my work will never end. I will never get everything done! As soon as I check one thing off my to-do list, I have to add something else. Will I ever be able to rest? You say I will. Your arms are everlasting. I may get tired, but You never do. I can rest in You. God, help me to seek You when my life feels out of control. Thank You for always being a safe place where I can find calm instead of chaos.

FEBRUARY 27

COLOSSIANS 3:2

*Set your minds on things above,
not on earthly things.*

God, when I set my mind on You, I am better at resisting sin. But my mind is easily distracted. Even when I start my day reading the Bible or praying, something else is always waiting to grab my attention. My friends need advice or I get asked out on a date or I get sucked into social media for hours. I need Your help to set my mind on You throughout my entire day, to come back to You when things are spinning around me. Help me to think of You when I am talking with others, when I need help with my chores, and even when I am scrolling through Instagram or watching funny videos on TikTok. Thank You for never leaving me. You are always there when I need You.

FEBRUARY 28

ISAIAH 45:5–6

"I am the LORD, and there is no other; there is no God but me. I will strengthen you, though you do not know me, so that all may know from the rising of the sun to its setting that there is no one but me. I am the LORD, and there is no other."

Dear Lord, You give me the strength to know You. The world says I should find what works best for me spiritually. When I hear about other faiths, I sometimes wonder what they are about. Could there be any truth to them? It's only because of You that I come to You. Even when I learn about the gods other people believe in, I remember there is no God like You. You are the only one who makes me happy—even on my worst days. You're the only one who left heaven to save people from their sins. Help me to believe You are better than anything the world tells me about. Thank You for always directing me back to You.

MARCH 1

1 JOHN 4:19, 21

We love because he first loved us. . . . And we have this command from him: The one who loves God must also love his brother and sister.

Jesus, You call me to love others the way You love me. But it's hard. I struggle to share my time and money with people who need it. Your love is selfless. Mine is selfish. You gave up everything. I get nervous about giving up anything. Jesus, Your love for me cost Your life. Will You help me serve people around me? Will you help me love my neighbors by mowing their lawns or taking out their garbage bins? Give me a heart that loves, even when it's uncomfortable or inconvenient. Thank You for loving me, Jesus.

MARCH 2

1 JOHN 2:17

And the world with its lust is passing away, but the one who does the will of God remains forever.

Father God, You tell me the things of this world will not last. But I still wish I had what other people have, and when I do, it changes the way I treat people. I either resent them for having something I want, or I use them to try and get what I want. But the things I want—a good reputation, the best stuff, popularity—will not last into eternity. Only my soul lasts. God, I want to follow You with all my heart and soul instead of chasing things. I want to consider people as people, not for what they have or don't have. Will You help me choose You over anything in the world? You are everything I could possibly want or need!

MARCH 3

PSALM 28:7

The LORD is my strength and my shield; my heart trusts in him, and I am helped. Therefore my heart celebrates, and I give thanks to him with my song.

Lord, trusting in You brings me such joy! But I spend most of my time chasing everything but You. I want to meet my parents' and teachers' expectations. When I don't, I feel like a failure. This verse helps me with those emotions. It says You are my shield. That means You protect me and are with me—even when I fail. You are my strength, too, whether I fail or succeed. Remembering that, I feel happy, because You are with me. Help me hold on to this joy always, Jesus. Thank You for always being my strength and shield! I am so glad You're mine.

MARCH 4

PSALM 46:10

"Stop fighting, and know that I am God, exalted among the nations, exalted on the earth."

King Jesus, when I feel like there are a hundred things I should be doing, I can be still and put my hope in You. I have such a hard time being still, though. It feels like if I'm not at school or with friends, I need to be on my phone or listening to music or doing anything to fill the silence. Before I know it, my mind is full of noise, and my schedule is controlling me. I haven't left any time to be quiet and still with You. Will You help me prioritize and become comfortable with stillness and silence? Thank You for Your calm voice throughout my chaotic days.

MARCH 5

ACTS 2:42

*They devoted themselves to the apostles'
teaching, to the fellowship, to the breaking
of bread, and to prayer.*

Dear God, I tend to base my friendships on shared interests or popularity. But Lord, I need friends who point me to You. I miss the point of friendship if I am only concerned with what we have in common or what I get out of them. Will You help me make friends with other Christians? Will You put people in my life who follow You with all their heart? Thank You for giving me friends who encourage me and help me grow closer to You!

MARCH 6

JEREMIAH 29:11

"For I know the plans I have for you"—this is the LORD's declaration—"plans for your well-being, not for disaster, to give you a future and a hope."

Father, thank You for Your plans for me! I have so many ideas about what I could do, from college or how much money I want to make one day to what I'm going to do this weekend. If I'm not careful, I try to run my life, forgetting Your plans are far better than mine. Help me remember You have good plans for my life, and help me to put my hope in what You have in store for me—not in what I think is best. Thank You for the way You have designed my life, in ways I can't even see yet!

MARCH 7

JOHN 6:37

"Everyone the Father gives me will come to me, and the one who comes to me I will never cast out."

Dear Jesus, I can come to You, no matter what I am struggling with, because You will never turn away. I sometimes wonder if You will, though. Maybe You will stop loving me because of my sin. And what if I keep sinning in the future? What if I fall into addiction or give into sexual temptations? Will You turn away because I haven't followed You like I should? But Jesus, You promise You will always be there, waiting patiently for me. You help me turn away from sin and follow You. Remind me that I am safe with You, especially when I am scared to come to You, Jesus. Thank You for welcoming me with open arms.

MARCH 8

EXODUS 34:6–7

The LORD—the LORD is a compassionate and gracious God, slow to anger and abounding in faithful love and truth, maintaining faithful love to a thousand generations, forgiving iniquity, rebellion, and sin.

Father in heaven, thank You for forgiving my sin! I sin against You over and over again, focusing on what I want instead of living for You. I choose popularity over telling people about Jesus. I choose a new phone or shoes over generosity. When I realize what I am doing, I feel guilty and completely unworthy of Your love. But You are compassionate and gracious. You tell me to return to You. You could become angry with me and punish me for my sin, but You forgive me, just like You've always done. Help me to turn away from sin, guilt, and shame, and follow You completely. Thank You for Your kindness.

NEW

MARCH 9

1 JOHN 3:18

*Little children, let us not love in word
or speech, but in action and in truth.*

Father God, I want to love others, not just with my words but with my actions, too. It's hard, though. Everyone says I should think of myself before I think of others. It's so easy to believe that message. I tell people I love them, but my actions prove I love myself. Will You help me overcome my selfishness? Will You give me a heart that loves my friends so much that I consider what they want first instead of second or last? Thank You for being the ultimate example of love and for helping me love.

MARCH 10

HEBREWS 5:7

During his earthly life, he [Jesus] offered prayers and appeals with loud cries and tears to the one who was able to save him from death, and he was heard because of his reverence.

King Jesus, thank You for showing me how to pray. Prayer is something I only think about doing when I really, really need You. I pray when I am scared, when I am nervous about a test or a doctor visit, and maybe when I am at church and someone reminds me to do it. But You prayed to God always, because You know Your Father's greatness. Jesus, I want to look to You as the example of how I should pray. Help me remember that I need You always. Guide me to pray like that's true. Thank You for showing me how I can talk with You.

MARCH 11

NEHEMIAH 9:6

You, LORD, are the only God. You created the heavens, the highest heavens with all their stars, the earth and all that is on it, the seas and all that is in them. You give life to all of them, and all the stars of heaven worship you.

Father God, it's easy to take Your creation for granted. I see things like the sun and the moon every day, and they rarely catch my attention. But when I stop to think about the miracle of creation, when I take in how intricate the universe is—I can't help but worship You. You are an artist! What a blessing to be among Your artwork! God, give me eyes to see Your creativity. Open my mouth to praise You every time I step into creation. Thank You for showing me a glimpse of Yourself through the things You've made. I am completely awestruck by Your creativity!

MARCH 12

PSALM 46:1

God is our refuge and strength,
a helper who is always found in times of trouble.

Lord God, You have always been my helper during hard times. Sometimes, though, I feel like You are far away from me. I turn to people for comfort. I can see them and hear them. They feel closer than You. But You're not far away. You are closer to me than anyone else at all, and You always have been. Will You remind me You are near when I am sad or angry or frustrated? Will You help me when I am in trouble? Thank You for being my helper in the past, God, and for being my helper always.

MARCH 13

PSALM 27:14

Wait for the LORD; be strong, and let your heart be courageous. Wait for the LORD.

God, I rarely need anything, but I really like having things when I want them. It's convenient. If I want to know something, I can learn about it almost immediately. If I want a warm meal, I can have it delivered. All of that makes waiting on You really hard. Will You help me be strong and courageous while I wait? Will You make me patient and help me put all my hope and trust in You even when it's hard or inconvenient? I know I grow when I wait on You, Lord. Thank You for making me more like You as I wait.

MARCH 14

PROVERBS 12:22

Lying lips are detestable to the LORD,
but faithful people are his delight.

Lord, You care about truth. But lying is pretty normal in my world. I hear kids talk about how to trick their parents or how to get away with drinking or smoking before school. If I'm honest, I am tempted to go along with them and make lying the norm in my life, too. But I don't want to be a liar, God. I want to be trustworthy. I want my words to delight You. Will You make me deeply uncomfortable with lying? Thank You for being the ultimate example of truth; You are truth.

MARCH 15

2 Corinthians 5:18

*Everything is from God, who has reconciled
us to himself through Christ and has given
us the ministry of reconciliation.*

God, thank You for making broken relationships right again! It's easy to resent someone who hurts me. I even want to hurt them back sometimes. Most people would probably agree I have a right to feel that way or act that way. But You died on the cross to repair my relationship with You and my relationships with other people. Will You help me heal broken relationships? Will You give me faith to persevere in mending what's damaged when the world tells me to walk away? Thank You for making my relationship with You right, and for giving me the strength to do the same with people around me.

MARCH 16

*The LORD my Lord is my strength;
he makes my feet like those of a deer and
enables me to walk on mountain heights!*

God, stepping into Your plans for my life is scary. I feel so weak and out of control! I don't like to go to places where I don't know anyone. I'm afraid when I think about everything I don't know about my future. But You say You're my strength. You always give me the strength to go where You lead, to walk into places I never thought possible. Give me courage I could never muster on my own. Help me remember I am not the one in control, and I never was. You are! You are God, and I am not. I want to follow You even when I am scared. Thank You for Your strength as I walk into Your plan.

MARCH 17

MATTHEW 6:6

"But when you pray, go into your private room, shut your door, and pray to your Father who is in secret. And your Father who sees in secret will reward you."

Lord, help me to remember my relationship with You isn't about impressing others. When I am around my Christian friends, I want to be seen as the person who follows You best. It's like I think that if I look like a perfect Christian to other people, I will somehow become one. Will You remind me my relationship with You isn't about showing off? Help me choose You, no matter who is watching me. Thank You for loving me when it's just You and me, and when it's You, me, and other people!

MARCH 18

So God created man in his own image;
he created him in the image of God;
he created them male and female.

Father of heaven, thank You for creating all people in Your image! The world tries to tell me some people are worth more than others, that they deserve better treatment because of their career, their popularity, what they look like, or where they live. If I'm not careful, I start to believe those things, even if it's just in the back of my mind. Will You help me view and treat people the way I want to be viewed and treated? Help me invite everyone in. I want to love people like they are made, loved, and treasured by You, because they are! I want to value people the same way You do. Thank You for making us in Your image!

MARCH 19

PSALM 22:1

My God, my God, why have you abandoned me?
Why are you so far from my deliverance
and from my words of groaning?

Lord God, when I can't feel You are close, I get scared. I think You might have abandoned me, and I am tempted to look for comfort in other places or from other people. Will You help me overcome that temptation? I want to draw closer to You. I know You are always there—You are always near to me, especially when I feel hopeless and alone. Remind me that You never leave. You give me the strength to cry out to You. Thank You for always being with me.

MARCH 20

If you keep silent at this time, relief and deliverance will come to the Jewish people from another place, but you and your father's family will be destroyed. Who knows, perhaps you have come to your royal position for such a time as this.

Father, thank You for placing me exactly where I am. It's so easy, though, to compare myself to others. I wonder why I am not as popular as my friends or why I don't have the same kinds of opportunities other people my age do. Some kids already make millions of dollars as influencers or are signed on to play sports in college. If I am not careful, I get jealous. I question if You are doing all You could be doing with my life. Help me remember Your plans are perfect, even if they don't always look the way I want them to. I praise You for placing me where I am. Thank You for how You are working in my life.

MARCH 21

LEVITICUS 19:18

Do not take revenge or bear a grudge against members of your community, but love your neighbor as yourself; I am the LORD.

Lord, when someone hurts me, You tell me to love them like I love myself. I confess I would rather hold a grudge. I am so scared of getting hurt again that I let bitterness into my heart. I start to build walls to keep people out. But bitterness and walls only lead me to hurt people back. You want me to act out of love, not bitterness. You want me to practice kindness, not grudge-holding. Help me love my friends the way You love me—the way I ultimately want to be loved. You never hold grudges against me for my sin. Thank You for helping me love people when they sin against me.

MARCH 22

PHILIPPIANS 1:9–10

And I pray this: that your love will keep on growing in knowledge and every kind of discernment, so that you may approve the things that are superior and may be pure and blameless in the day of Christ.

Holy Spirit, help me accept Your will for my life. I know it will be hard. I usually choose my own path instead of Yours. I watch shows that lead my mind away from Your truth or go along with what my friends are doing instead of valuing what You say is good. I just want to fit in—and that sometimes becomes more important than obeying You. I make decisions without asking what You want. Will You remind me that the best thing I can do is to love You? Show me You know best. Keep growing me in the knowledge of God and His ways. Thank You for leading me and helping me follow You.

MARCH 23

PSALM 1:1–2

How happy is the one who does not walk in the advice of the wicked or stand in the pathway with sinners or sit in the company of mockers! Instead, his delight is in the LORD's instruction, and he meditates on it day and night.

God, a thousand messages bombard me all the time, many of them telling me to put myself above everyone else. They say it's okay to build my "image," to define myself by how I compare with everyone else, and to chase happiness. But Your Word tells me something different. It says that when I look to You and Your instruction, I will find something lasting—eternal delight! God, give me a desire to study Your Word and to seek the joy that comes from You. Thank You for speaking to me through the Bible. Your Word brings delight!

MARCH 24

MATTHEW 3:2

*"Repent, because the kingdom
of heaven has come near!"*

Jesus, You say to repent of my sin, but I struggle to obey. I know You were punished for all my sin, in my place—so why do I choose to disobey You? It's like I have become numb to some of my sins. Or I get focused on my happiness as being the most important thing. I don't even consider the effects of what I'm doing. Will You help me look to You? Transform my mind, Jesus. Take away any satisfaction that sin brings. I want to live with eternity in mind. Thank You for Your patience and grace as I keep repenting from sin and seek to become more like You.

MARCH 25

HEBREWS 10:24

*And let us consider one another in order to
provoke love and good works.*

God, when one of my friends is going through
something hard, it's easier to say I'll pray for them
instead of asking what I can do. I forget You want
me to help others with my hands and feet, not
just encourage them with my words. You want me
to serve my friends with good deeds. Help me to
combine prayer with acts of love, and give me a willingness to sacrifice my own comfort so that other
people can feel Your kindness. Thank You for teaching me how to love my friends through my actions.

MARCH 26

MATTHEW 11:28

"Come to me, all of you who are weary and burdened, and I will give you rest."

Jesus, I praise You. I can place my burdens on You, because there is nothing too heavy for You. Still, I feel pressure to put on a happy face when I am sad or anxious. I fear that if I show people how I am really feeling, they might think less of me and push me away. When people ask, "How are you?" I say "I'm fine," without even thinking about it, even when it's the furthest thing from the truth. Lord, help me remember that I never have to put on a brave face for You. There is no emotion I feel that will cause You to turn away from me. You promise to bear my burdens; I just need to bring them to You. Thank You for shouldering my burdens no matter how big they are, Jesus.

MARCH 27

PROVERBS 14:29

A patient person shows great understanding, but a quick-tempered one promotes foolishness.

Father, my quick temper gets me in trouble! It never serves me like I think it will. When I feel wronged by someone, my anger spills out with words or actions I can't take back. That's not how You want me to act. You want me to love others by being patient and kind in all circumstances. Give me understanding when my friends confuse or frustrate me. I want to point people to You by acting wisely rather than foolishly. I praise You for giving me the ability to choose patience over anger, God. I know that comes only from You.

MARCH 28

PHILIPPIANS 2:15

*So that you may be blameless and pure,
children of God who are faultless in a crooked
and perverted generation, among whom you
shine like stars in the world.*

God, You want me to shine in a dark world so others can see You. When sin is all around me, I don't always stand out. I blend in. I join in the sin or just stay quiet. I am afraid to stick out, but I don't want to be afraid anymore. I want to shine Your light in such a way that I point people to You. Give me courage to obey You and to tell people You are the rescuer. Thank You for being the Light who brings true hope. Thank You for shining through me, into the world.

MARCH 29

JAMES 1:2–4

*Consider it a great joy, my brothers and sisters,
whenever you experience various trials,
because you know that the testing of
your faith produces endurance. And let
endurance have its full effect, so that you
may be mature and complete, lacking nothing.*

Lord, thank You for using everything in my life—even the hard things—to help me look more like Jesus. I confess suffering and hardship seem random and pointless to me. I sometimes believe You are only in the happy things, that You are absent from anything bad. I feel so alone when I believe that lie. Help me remember what the book of James says. Whenever I am sick or lonely, hungry or misunderstood, You are present. You see everything that happens in this world and in my life. Nothing is random or pointless. You use the hard things in my life to make me grow. Thank You for being in everything, Lord, the good and the bad.

MARCH 30

2 Peter 1:4

By these he has given us very great and precious promises, so that through them you may share in the divine nature, escaping the corruption that is in the world because of evil desire.

Father God, You never break Your promises. That's amazing! I can't imagine being so trustworthy that I never break a promise to anyone. It seems like I struggle to keep the promises I make. I constantly let down the people I love most. That's one reason why You are so amazing to me. You always fulfill Your promises. Help me look to You as the one I can fully count on. Help me become more trustworthy, like You are trustworthy. Thank You for never letting me down or never breaking a promise.

MARCH 31

MARK 12:29–31

Jesus answered, "The most important is Listen, Israel! The Lord our God, the Lord is one. Love the Lord your God with all your heart, with all your soul, with all your mind, and with all your strength. The second is, Love your neighbor as yourself. There is no other command greater than these."

Lord God, it is amazing that loving You helps me love others. Even though those two things are connected, I tend to focus on my relationship with You. I neglect my relationships with others. When I see an opportunity to love someone, my first question is, "Do I have time for this?" instead of "How would I like to be loved?" That isn't love at all! It's actually evidence I am not following You the way I should. Help me to love other people as much as You do. Thank You, God, for placing Your amazing love on me. I want my love for others to flow out of my relationship with You.

APRIL 1

PROVERBS 24:16

Though a righteous person falls seven times, he will get up, but the wicked will stumble into ruin.

Father in heaven, I know I will not follow You 100 percent of the time. Sometimes I get distracted by what everyone else is doing. It's easy to drift. I stop thinking about how my choices reflect You to people around me, and I stop speaking like You are in the room with me. I turn away from You and act like I haven't been saved by Your grace. But my failure isn't final. You always give me the opportunity to come back to You. Help me see all my failures as opportunities to turn around and follow You again. Thank You for Your grace that makes me grow stronger in my faith.

APRIL 2

"If your presence does not go," Moses responded to him, "don't make us go up from here."

God, I don't want to be anywhere that doesn't honor You. If I'm given the chance, I chase success the way the world tells me to instead of following You. I sometimes believe my joy comes from what I can do on my own—without You. But I know there is no true happiness if You're not with me. I want to be like Moses: unwilling to chase anything in this world if it means You won't be there. Give me a willingness to trade every good thing on earth for being with You.

APRIL 3

1 JOHN 3:1

See what great love the Father has given us that we should be called God's children— and we are! The reason the world does not know us is that it didn't know him.

Father God, I know I care way too much about what my friends think of me. It's nice to feel appreciated, and I want to please my friends and family. When I let people down, it's more than just disappointment. I become so disheartened that I question my value. Will You remind me my worth comes from You? Help me remember my identity isn't defined by what anyone thinks of me—it's found in my adoption into Your family. I am Your child. Your love is so amazing, God! Thank You for not loving me because of my own goodness, God, but because of Yours.

APRIL 4

1 PETER 2:21

For you were called to this, because Christ also suffered for you, leaving you an example, that you should follow in his steps.

Jesus, I know I am supposed to imitate You. But I often want to be like everyone else. Or I forget to look to You, focusing instead on all the people I can follow on social media. I start to model my life after theirs instead of Yours. I start believing the people on social media are always right. I model my life after theirs instead of yours; I believe the people on social media are always right; I follow my heart, expressing my sexuality however I want; and I disobey my parents if I think it will make me happy. Will You help me resist that temptation? Give me the strength to imitate You. Grow within me the desire to know and love You so well that I can't help but act just like You. Thank You for having the best footsteps to follow; help me to walk in them!

APRIL 5

PHILIPPIANS 4:8

Finally brothers and sisters, whatever is true, whatever is honorable, whatever is just, whatever is pure, whatever is lovely, whatever is commendable—if there is any moral excellence and if there is anything praiseworthy—dwell on these things.

God, You want me to focus on true and lovely things. It's hard to know what is true and lovely, though. Some of my teachers say truth isn't real: "Just because something is true for you," they say, "does not mean it's true for someone else." But when truth isn't truth, what do I trust? Who do I trust? Your Word says I can trust You, because You are truth. Help me focus on You, the truth. Give me wisdom to know when the world is lying to me. I praise You because You hold all truth. I can hold fast to everything You say, because You are trustworthy.

NEW

APRIL 6

ISAIAH 54:10

"Though the mountains move and the hills shake, my love will not be removed from you and my covenant of peace will not be shaken," says your compassionate LORD.

Father God, Your presence brings me peace. When I am not following You, I search for calm in places where I will never find it. I look for it in my friends, but no matter how hard we try, we let each other down. I look for it in my grades or trophies, but no matter how well I do, there is always something more to achieve or accomplish. There is nowhere I can rest on this earth where I won't be disappointed, let down, or told to stop resting and work harder. Help me to stop looking for peace in anything but You. Your presence is the only place where peace is constant and sure. Thank You for being my resting place, God.

APRIL 7

ROMANS 8:25

Now if we hope for what we do not see, we eagerly wait for it with patience.

Lord, thank You that I can count on You to answer my prayers. Waiting for an answer is hard. Usually, when I want to know something, I can just search for it. I can go to the Internet or ask a friend or family member. Waiting patiently is difficult! But I know that even when I am waiting, You are working. Will You help me to be a more patient person? Give me confidence that You will answer me. Then help me trust Your answer, even if it's "no" or "not yet." Thank You that I can come to You for Your good and perfect answer to every prayer I pray.

APRIL 8

JAMES 1:27

Pure and undefiled religion before God the Father is this: to look after orphans and widows in their distress and to keep oneself unstained from the world.

Jesus, You tell Christians to serve the most vulnerable people—widows and orphans, the homeless. I confess I get so caught up in my own problems that I can't see anyone else's. And while You care about what I am going through, You instruct me to care for people. Instead of obsessing over my problems, help me see vulnerable people around me. Shift my focus from solving my problems to loving other people. Give me eyes to see people the way You see them, and to treat them like You would, even if it means putting my troubles aside for a while. Thank You for putting my needs before Yours. Help me be willing to do the same for other people.

APRIL 9

1 SAMUEL 16:7

But the LORD said to Samuel, "Do not look at his appearance or his stature because I have rejected him. Humans do not see what the LORD sees, for humans see what is visible, but the LORD sees the heart."

God, Your standard of beauty isn't like everyone else's. People look at the outside, and I am tempted to do the same. I judge based on outward appearance before getting to know people. And—I can be obsessed with what people think about my appearance, too. But when You look at me, one of Your children, You see the beautiful holiness of Jesus. Give me eyes to see beauty as You do. Help me reflect Jesus's beauty instead of what Instagram or magazines say is beautiful. Thank You for looking at the inside first and for being concerned about my heart.

NEW

APRIL 10

PSALM 139:1–2

LORD, you have searched me and known me. You know when I sit down and when I stand up; you understand my thoughts from far away.

God, it's amazing that You know me even better than I know myself. You know what I am going to do before I do. I like to pretend You aren't looking when I sin—like my sins are hidden from You. I try to sneak around as if You're not with me, but You are always there. You're there when I am at church on Sunday, and You're there when I choose to party with my friends on Saturday night. Through it all, You keep asking me to leave my sin, even when I act like I can't hear You. Help me come to You instead of running away from You. Thank You for loving me even though You know my deepest, darkest sins.

APRIL 11

PSALM 32:7

*You are my hiding place; you protect
me from trouble. You surround me
with joyful shouts of deliverance.*

God, when life is hard, I can come close to You. I don't like pain and sadness, though. They feel like punishment. I start to wonder what I did to deserve this pain and heartache. If I'm not careful, I begin to question if You are good. I think about running away from You instead of coming to You, my hiding place. When I am in pain or sad, I should run toward You. That's what I want to do, Lord! Help me to embrace hardships as opportunities to come close to You. Give me comfort while I wait for joy to come again. Thank You for being with me in every situation.

APRIL 12

HEBREWS 4:15

*For we do not have a high priest who
is unable to sympathize with our weaknesses,
but one who has been tempted in every
way as we are, yet without sin.*

Jesus, when I am tempted to sin, I often think You wouldn't understand—if anyone were in my shoes, they would do the same thing I would choose to do. But You didn't. You experienced temptations like I do and said "no" to sin. You resisted every temptation. I can do the same because You are helping me! Help me come to You when I am tempted to sin. You have sympathy for my weakness, and You help me choose to follow You. You show me grace I don't deserve! Thank You for understanding my weakness. You are such a kind God.

APRIL 13

1 CORINTHIANS 1:9

God is faithful; you were called by him into fellowship with his Son, Jesus Christ our Lord.

Father, You are faithful, even when I am faithless. I go through seasons when all my focus goes to things other than You: schoolwork, friends, what I am doing after school—the list goes on. It's like I can only pay attention to the things I can experience with my five senses. I lose sight of You and end up choosing You mostly when I feel like it. But I know You are there, God. Help me to be faithful to You in all my life, just like You are to me. I praise You that You aren't just with me when I'm being a "good" Christian. You are dependable all the time.

APRIL 14

GENESIS 16:13

So she [Hagar] named the LORD who spoke to her: "You are El-roi," for she said, "In this place, have I actually seen the one who sees me?"

God, You are the only one who sees me completely. When I am suffering or hurting, it feels like no one else can relate to what I'm going through. I am the only one who feels the things I feel. It's lonely and frustrating, and sometimes it's easier to pretend I'm not hurting at all. But You see me like no one else does or can. You know my pain better than anyone else. When I feel cut off from the rest of the world, will You remind me that You are the God who sees? Thank You for seeing me in my pain and for allowing me to come to You when my heart hurts.

APRIL 15

PROVERBS 9:9

*Instruct the wise, and he will be wiser still;
teach the righteous, and he will learn more.*

Lord, I can't grow wise if I keep comparing myself to other people. If anyone knows more than me, I try to prove I am better than them by answering questions faster or talking about how well I did on a test. I spend so much time giving into that pressure that I struggle to see people as anything other than competition. But You want me to be humble and wise. Help me to stop comparing myself with the people You have placed in my life. You have given them to me so I can learn! Thank You for being the best teacher of all time.

APRIL 16

*But those who trust in the LORD will renew
their strength; they will soar on wings
like eagles; they will run and not become
weary, they will walk and not faint.*

God, when I am tired, You give me strength.
Sometimes I think I should pretend to be perfect.
I wish I were. It would be nice to never sin or have
any bad thoughts and to always trust You without
question. But I am weak, God. When I reach for
perfection, I just get tired. Help me admit my weakness instead of pretending I'm perfect. You are my
strength. I could never be strong enough to follow
You all by myself, so I'm giving You all the glory!
Thank You for giving me strength to live for You.

APRIL 17

ROMANS 5:5

This hope will not disappoint us, because God's love has been poured out in our hearts through the Holy Spirit who was given to us.

Holy Spirit, You help me feel God's love for me. Even when nothing is going right around me, I know You are with me. But I don't always think that way. When my family life isn't perfect, I think, If You really loved me, You would change that. When I am not as good at sports or choir or art as my friends, I wonder why I'm not the best. Is it because I have done something wrong? Is it because You love someone else more than me? But it's in those moments, You whisper I am loved. Remind me that Your love isn't because of what I do—it's because of how great You are. Thank You for loving me even though You don't have to!

APRIL 18

ISAIAH 26:3

You will keep the mind that is dependent on you in perfect peace, for it is trusting in you.

Father in heaven, I know I don't have to feel overwhelmed. You give me perfect peace, no matter what's going on in my life. But I sometimes feel so sad that I wonder if I will ever feel peaceful again. My sadness overshadows everything. When I focus on it and not on You, I lose the peace that comes from You. It's still there, though, because You're there. Help me turn to You when sadness overwhelms me. Remind me that Your peace is always waiting for me, even when I can't see it or feel it. Thank You for giving me rest and peace.

COLOSSIANS 2:6–7

So then, just as you have received Christ Jesus as Lord, continue to walk in him, being rooted and built up in him and established in the faith, just as you were taught, and overflowing with gratitude.

Jesus, when I complain and grumble, I don't look like You. I confess I get jealous and frustrated when someone has something I want. I wonder why I haven't been blessed as much as they have. Then I complain about it to other people or just in my own heart. Ugh. That's not like You at all! You—the creator of everything—came to earth and were treated like nothing. You never complained. You always were gracious and kind. Jesus, I want to reflect You. Help me to be thankful instead of grumbling. Thank You for Your grace!

APRIL 20

MARK 10:15–16

"Truly I tell you, whoever does not receive the kingdom of God like a little child will never enter it." After taking them in his arms, he laid his hands on them and blessed them.

God, it takes childlike faith to trust You. It's hard, though. Some of my friends and teachers say I should stop putting my faith in You—that You didn't create the world and that people are random accidents. It seems like I hear messages pointing me away from You all the time. Help me put my trust in You like a child trusts a loving parent. Give me confidence and courage to reject any message that tells me faith in You is foolish. Thank You for welcoming me, Your child, with open arms. I'm so glad You're my Father!

APRIL 21

JEREMIAH 33:3

Call to me and I will answer you and tell you great and incomprehensible things you do not know.

Lord God, You always lead me in the right direction! In the past, I have gone with the flow without question. When I see everyone else doing something, I follow them without asking what You think. The truth is, I am scared to walk away from the crowd. What will people think of me? Will I still fit in? But You promise You will always lead me where I need to go—even if it's in the opposite direction from other people. Help me trust You as I listen to what You say is right and good. Thank You for helping me follow You.

APRIL 22

ISAIAH 41:10

Do not fear, for I am with you; do not be afraid, for I am your God. I will strengthen you; I will help you; I will hold on to you with my righteous right hand.

God in heaven, when I feel down or depressed, You are my safe place. But it can be hard to worship You when I feel low. I get so wrapped up in my feelings that I can't see Your goodness. Help me declare You are wonderful, no matter how I am feeling. You see me in my sadness; help me see You and give thanks. You see me in my gladness; help me see You and give thanks. You are worthy of worship at all times and in all places! You are so kind to me as I learn how to worship You with my emotions. I praise You for always being my safe place.

APRIL 23

A tranquil heart is life to the body,
but jealousy is rottenness to the bones.

Father, You use gratitude to take away my jealousy. When I notice all the things I don't have, I feel like I am missing out. I wonder why I don't have what everyone else has. I forget everything You have given me: my life, the people You have put around me, and the greatest gift of all—being part of Your family! God, I need You to help me become more grateful. Help me let go of jealousy. Thank You for always giving me exactly what I need.

APRIL 24

ECCLESIASTES 7:9

*Don't let your spirit rush to be angry,
for anger abides in the heart of fools.*

Lord, I know it's wise to think about the consequences of my actions before I act, but sometimes, I let my temper control me. I give into anger. I let it out on social media; I even let it control who I am friends with. Sometimes, it determines how I feel about You. I get angry with You when something doesn't go my way. But my anger has consequences, and I don't want it to run my life. Give me wisdom to think before I act. I am so grateful that You are patient with me as I learn to control my anger.

APRIL 25

PSALM 5:3

*In the morning, LORD, you hear my voice;
in the morning I plead my case
to you and watch expectantly.*

Father, You hear and answer my prayers. How amazing that is! But I sometimes wonder if You are really listening to me. How could one God hear all the prayers of all His children at once? How could You care about my problems? They seem so small compared to the bigger things going on in the world. Sometimes those thoughts control me, and I stop talking with You. But Your Word tells me You hear me, and it says I can expect You to answer me. Thank You for always being trustworthy, for always listening to me, and for always caring about what I am going through. I will pray expectantly, like how I wait for gifts on my birthday or at Christmas, because You hear me.

APRIL 26

PROVERBS 10:11

The mouth of the righteous is a fountain of life,
but the mouth of the wicked conceals violence.

Jesus, encouragement from other Christians is the best kind of encouragement! It always makes me feel alive. Sometimes, though, I listen to people who don't follow You. I want to be reassured that what I am doing or thinking isn't wrong—even when I know it is. Will You place Christians in my life who encourage me to follow You? Thank You for their encouragement. They comfort me when I feel weak, convict me when I am headed the wrong direction in life, and inspire me to follow You with every part of me.

APRIL 27

MATTHEW 10:30

*"But even the hairs of your
head have all been counted."*

God, You know every part of me so well. You even know how many hairs I have on my head! That's amazing. I can't really understand it—how do You know every detail about me, even things I don't know? It doesn't make sense. Shouldn't I know myself? But I definitely don't know how many hairs are on my head. Only You do! If you know that about me, You must know what's best for me. Help me to believe that truth and to trust You with every part of my being. Thank You for taking such an interest in me that You know every detail about my life.

AMEN

APRIL 28

MATTHEW 18:21–22

*Then Peter approached him and asked,
"Lord, how many times must I forgive
my brother or sister who sins against
me? As many as seven times?"
"I tell you, not as many as seven,"
Jesus replied, "but seventy times seven."*

God, some people are hard to love. They are mean or rude to me, and I just want to step away from them. But a lot of them don't know Your love and forgiveness, so how can I expect them to love me the way You do? Plus, if I'm honest, I am hard to love sometimes, too. It's one of the reasons I'm so thankful for Your love and forgiveness! Help me forgive people, even when I don't want to or when it's inconvenient and uncomfortable. Thank You for loving me when I am hard to love, and thank You for helping me share Your kindness with others.

APRIL 29

JOHN 14:27

"Peace I leave with you. My peace I give to you. I do not give to you as the world gives. Don't let your heart be troubled or fearful."

Jesus Christ, when everything seems out of control, You bring peace. Sometimes I feel like the weight of the whole world is on my shoulders, especially when I try to please people, even good people like my teachers, friends, and family. But when I try to be everything that everyone expects of me, I start to feel like I am spinning out of control. Jesus, when I can't catch my breath, pull me close and calm my heart. Remind me that I am not capable of meeting everybody's expectations. That's a good thing! It helps me rely on You every day. When I feel out of control, Jesus, give me a peace that can't come from anywhere but You. I am in awe of how You calm my restless mind and heart, Jesus.

APRIL 30

LUKE 6:46

*"Why do you call me 'Lord, Lord,'
and don't do the things I say?"*

God, I want to love You by obeying You. Too often, though, I say that You are my God but live like I don't know You. I talk like my friends talk, or I disrespect my parents, or I am mean to a friend or sibling. I want to obey You with every part of my life—in Bible study, at church, with my family, and when I am with my friends. Help me love You through the way I live, Lord. I praise You for being so kind to me. Even when I disobey You, You keep inviting me to love and obey You every day.

MAY 1

JOSHUA 1:9

"Haven't I commanded you: be strong and courageous? Do not be afraid or discouraged, for the LORD your God is with you wherever you go."

Dear God, thank You for being with me! It feels like my life is constantly changing, and I'm never ready for it. Whether I am starting a new year in school, trying out a new activity, or getting ready for a friend to move away—I feel like I can't handle all the change. I become afraid I won't like the next stage of my life. Maybe it will be harder or scarier or lonelier. I get so discouraged that I think nothing new can ever be good. But Your Word says I don't have to be discouraged or scared. You are with me always. Will You help me be strong and courageous? Thank You for never leaving me!

MAY 2

1 JOHN 4:8

The one who does not love does not know God, because God is love.

Father God, You define love. You are love! In the past, I have believed that love is all about how I feel. If I am happy when I'm with my friends, that must mean they love me. The minute they make me upset, though, I question their love. I wonder if their love was ever real in the first place. But God, You tell me love *isn't* a feeling. It's a commitment, and there has been no better commitment than Your love for Your children. I can't count on love if it's a feeling, because even my feelings let me down. Help me be happy in Your love, and help me show Your love to others by treating them like You would. Thank You, Lord, for Your amazing, committed love!

MAY 3

EXODUS 9:16

*However, I have let you live for this purpose:
to show you my power and to make my name
known on the whole earth.*

God, thank You for using me to make Your name known! So many times, I choose not to share You with others, even with an opportunity right in front of me. I shy away from the conversation or change the subject because I am afraid of what someone will think of me. Help me to stop being shy and start being brave. Give me such confidence in Your power that I can't help but shout Your name from the rooftops! Thank You for including me in Your purpose to make Your name known on the whole earth, even though I have been scared to speak of You in the past. I am trusting You for boldness!

MAY 4

MATTHEW 10:14

"If anyone does not welcome you or listen to your words, shake the dust off your feet when you leave that house or town."

Lord, Your Word says not everyone will want to hear about You. When I am sharing Your good news with others, I take it personally if they reject You. I get embarrassed and start making it all about me instead of all about You. *Was it the way I said something? What do they think of me?* I don't want to talk about You in an attempt to impress other people; I want to be someone who honors You with my words instead of honoring myself. Give me the courage to tell people about You, because I know it's the truth. Help me to know a rejection of You isn't a rejection of me. Remind me that I cannot please everyone, no matter how good the news about You is, and I don't have to try. Thank You for humbling me as I share the good news about You.

MAY 5

ECCLESIASTES 1:14

I have seen all the things that are done under the sun and have found everything to be futile, a pursuit of the wind.

Father, nothing on this earth will last for eternity. I know this is true, but I still act like my stuff is the most important thing on this earth. When I don't have phones or clothes or headphones that are the newest and greatest, I get embarrassed. I see people who have the things I want, and I wonder why I can't have them, too. My mind can't stop thinking about everything I want even though none of it will last. I'll have to replace it, or I'll want something else. Help me to focus on the things that last, God. I want to see the things of this world as things that will wear out. They won't ever last. They aren't eternal, like You are. I want to value You and the people You have created. Thank You for Your eternal, everlasting, unfading love. It will go with me all the way into eternity!

MAY 6

PROVERBS 18:21

*Death and life are in the power of the tongue,
and those who love it will eat its fruit.*

God, it is such a big responsibility to know that my words can bring both joy and pain. I don't think about that enough. I tend to say whatever comes to mind without considering how it'll make someone feel. It only takes a second for words to leave my mouth, but those words last so much longer. People have said things to me I still remember: words that were encouraging and words that were hurtful. Help me think before I speak, God. Make me an encourager instead of a discourager. I want to be someone who builds up people, not someone who tears them down. Your words give me life! Thank You for reminding me to do the same with the words I speak to others.

MAY 7

PHILIPPIANS 2:3–4

Do nothing out of selfish ambition or conceit, but in humility consider others as more important than yourselves. Everyone should look not to his own interests, but rather to the interests of others.

Dear Jesus, I want to focus on other people more than I focus on myself. I spend a lot of time thinking about how I can be the best in my class, the top scorer at soccer, or the favorite grandkid. I know You want me to work hard at everything I do. But, God, I can get so wrapped up in *me* that I forget about everyone else. If I am being honest, I don't know how to remember both me *and* the people in my life. Will You help me do that even though I don't know how? Give me eyes to see what people need. Help me be more concerned with others than I am with myself. Thank You for loving me so much that You died for me. Help me love people the same way You love me.

MAY 8

PROVERBS 12:15

A fool's way is right in his own eyes,
but whoever listens to counsel is wise.

God, it's amazing Your wisdom can come through people's advice! Sometimes when my parents or teachers tell me what to do, my pride gets the best of me. I think they will steer me in the wrong direction, because they don't know me well enough. I believe I am right, so I don't listen when I am corrected. Help me know when to stop speaking and start listening. I know You have given me friends, family, teachers, and other people to speak to me and get my attention. Thank You, God, for every voice You use to speak into my life!

MAY 9

PSALM 54:4

God is my helper;
the Lord is the sustainer of my life.

God, I need to remember how You've helped me in my sin. Sinning against You can be so normal that I don't even realize I am doing it. I have certain sins I can't shake—especially when they don't seem like that big of a deal to me. I tell white lies to my parents or bad-mouth people who make me mad. I want to stop doing these things, but I can't do it on my own. I need You to help me, God. Remind me how You have helped me beat sin in the past so I can overcome sin now. You are stronger and more powerful than every one of my sins! You have always been so faithful to me. Thank You for never leaving me in my sin, no matter how many times I fail to follow You.

MAY 10

MATTHEW 7:1–2

"Do not judge, so that you won't be judged. For you will be judged by the same standard with which you judge others, and you will be measured by the same measure you use."

Lord, You give me power to show mercy to people when I don't really want to. I can be so critical of others. When I see people making choices I wouldn't, I start to judge them. I become unkind and distant. The truth is, I deserve to be criticized for my own sin, God, but You show me kindness instead. You don't scold me. You don't shame me, either, so why do I shame other people? Will You help me offer mercy instead of judgment? I praise You, God! You died for my sins. You give me grace, not guilt. Keep reminding me of Your mercy so I can give it to other people.

MAY 11

PSALM 119:52

*LORD, I remember your judgments
from long ago and find comfort.*

God, I find such comfort in Your Word. But sometimes, I listen for You and can't hear You. I pray, but You don't speak back. I want to know, exactly, what I should do or how I should feel. When I don't hear anything, I feel like You're not there or that You're not listening. But when my heart says I can't hear You, all I have to do is open my Bible. Help me remember Your words in the Bible are Your words in my life. The Bible helps me know how to think and feel and what to do. I am so thankful that when I need help, You are always there. You speak to me through Your Bible.

MAY 12

PSALM 33:20

We wait for the LORD;
he is our help and shield.

Father, I wait for You, because You are my help. In the past, I have been so impatient. I rush ahead, doing what I want to do, when I want to do it, instead of trusting You. But that's not how You want me to live. You want me to wait for You! Help me trust You with everything. Teach me to come to You first—before going to other people or following my gut. Give me patience to wait on You when You don't answer me right away or when You answer in a way I don't want or expect. Even when I choose to do things my way, You lovingly call me back to You. Thank You for protecting me and helping me as I wait for You.

MAY 13

AMEN

PSALM 94:18–19

*If I say, "My foot is slipping,"
your faithful love will support me, LORD.
When I am filled with cares,
your comfort brings me joy.*

God, when I feel out of control, I can focus on You. In my mind, I think I can hold everything together. I think that if I can control my future—my grades, who I will or won't date, where I go to school—everything will go right for me. But I get things wrong all the time. You are the only one who is in control of everything. When I stress about what I can't control, help me seek You. Give me peace. You hold all things, including all my decisions and circumstances, in Your loving hands. Thank You for Your eternal presence, and thank You for holding everything together.

MAY 14

GALATIANS 1:7

*There are some who are troubling you
and want to distort the gospel of Christ.*

Jesus, so many people in my life aren't interested in You as Savior. They tell me I can save myself, that I should trust my heart. But my heart can be reckless, immature, and unkind. I don't trust my heart, Lord. Without Your help, I would think of myself before I think of anyone or anything else. Jesus, I need You to be my Savior. You're the only one who has the power to forgive sins! Help me to reject the message that I can save myself. You have rescued me! Thank You for saving me from my sins.

MAY 15

1 PETER 2:2–3

Like newborn infants, desire the pure milk of the word, so that by it you may grow up into your salvation, if you have tasted that the Lord is good.

God, You are the only one I need to grow in my faith! No other god or belief system can make me more like You. I've heard I can take little pieces of every belief system to make something that works *for me*—that I can take the parts I like and leave out what I don't—to become my "best self." Help me reject that idea. Only You make me grow. Help me to stop searching for what makes me feel like a "better person" and to trust You to make me more like Your Son. I praise You for helping me become a little more like You.

NEW

MAY 16

GENESIS 1:1

*In the beginning God created
the heavens and the earth.*

Lord God, You created everything! When I look at this earth and think about how fragile it is, I get scared. Tornadoes, fires, and hurricanes can rip apart a town in hours or even minutes. I love Your creation, but I am also terrified of what it can do. Give me peace. Remind me nothing is outside of Your control. You created everything, *and* You hold it all together! Help me see and remember the beauty in creation. Help me depend on You, too, even when storms and natural disasters happen. Thank You for giving me a beautiful world to live in.

MAY 17

MATTHEW 7:3–4

"Why do you look at the splinter in your brother's eye but don't notice the beam of wood in your own eye? Or how can you say to your brother, 'Let me take the splinter out of your eye,' and look, there's a beam of wood in your own eye?"

Jesus, before I judge others, I need to take a hard look at myself. I am so quick to criticize people for their sin when I barely notice my own. If I am being honest, I judge people to make myself feel better. I don't want to feel bad about my sin. But I know that to follow You, I need to examine the sin in my life. Will You give me the ability to see and fight my sin? I want to take the log out of my eye, like You ask me to do in Your Word. Thank You for showing me why I tend to focus on other people's sin rather than my own. Thank You for helping me see my sin so I can fight it and become more like You.

MAY 18

ROMANS 8:37

No, in all these things we are more than conquerors through him who loved us.

King Jesus, You have given me victory in my fight against sin! That truth fills me with such hope, because sometimes the fight feels impossible. I get caught in cycles of sin. I disobey You once—and then I do it again and again. Before I know it, I am sinning without even thinking about it. And it's not just a one-time thing anymore; it's become a sin habit. Help me remember I cannot fight sin on my own and win, Jesus. Remind me to ask You for help. You conquered sin, and through Your conquering power, I receive the ability to overcome even my worst repeated sins. Thank You for defeating sin! Thank You that, because of Your death and resurrection, a day is coming in which I will never sin again.

MAY 19

PSALM 119:1–3

How happy are those whose way is blameless,who walk according to the LORD's instruction! Happy are those who keep his decrees and seek him with all their heart. They do nothing wrong;they walk in his ways.

Dear God, thank You for Your Word! I don't always turn to the Bible for answers. It's easier to ask my friends for advice or to just go with what feels right. But when I ignore or forget Your Word, I make the wrong choices. Throughout the Bible, You have spoken and told me how I should live. Help me turn to Your Word so I can make choices that honor You. I want to treasure Your Word so I turn to You when I need help. Thank You, God, for giving me Your instructions in the Bible!

MAY 20

JOHN 15:16

"You did not choose me, but I chose you. I appointed you to go and produce fruit and that your fruit should remain, so that whatever you ask the Father in my name, he will give you."

Father God, even when I don't like myself, You like me. I have no idea why You would choose someone like me—You know the deepest parts of my heart, and sometimes it's not very pretty. Other times I feel like a fake. How can I be a Christian when I think and say and do the things I do? Help me trust in Your love, God. You didn't choose me based on how good I am or how strong I am when I'm tempted to disobey You. I don't really know why You chose me, but You did. You love me! Help me rest in Your love even when I feel unworthy of it. Thank You for choosing to know and love me as Your child.

MAY 21

JOSHUA 10:13

And the sun stood still and the moon stopped until the nation took vengeance on its enemies. Isn't this written in the Book of Jashar? So the sun stopped in the middle of the sky and delayed its setting almost a full day.

Lord, nothing can stand in the way of Your purposes! If You want to stop the sun, You can! I sometimes believe my choices can ruin Your plans, and I get scared of making the wrong ones. What if I choose the wrong path for my future? What if one bad choice wrecks my whole life? In these moments, I am trusting myself more than You. I believe my ability to mess up Your plans is stronger than Your good plans. Help me remember nothing can stand in the way of what You intend to do—not even my worst or best choice. Help me to make decisions based on faith in You, not my fear of what could happen. Thank You for being stronger than anything and everything!

MAY 22

MATTHEW 6:19–21

"Don't store up for yourselves treasures on earth, where moth and rust destroy and where thieves break in and steal. But store up for yourselves treasures in heaven, where neither moth nor rust destroys, and where thieves don't break in and steal. For where your treasure is, there your heart will be also."

Lord, sometimes my heart becomes greedy. I want to hold on to things of this world, even though they aren't eternal. Other times, I compare what I have to others and feel jealous when I don't measure up. If I don't wear the right clothes, I wonder what people think of me. And when I don't make the best grades or do well in sports, I wonder if I will be any good at anything. Will You help me push past these things and look at Your gifts? Turn my heart to You when I am unhappy. I want to be grateful, and I can be. When I treasure eternal things, I honor You, the giver of all good gifts. God, help my heart treasure You more than anything else on earth.

MAY 23

ECCLESIASTES 3:11

He has made everything appropriate in its time. He has also put eternity in their hearts, but no one can discover the work God has done from beginning to end.

God, You created me for eternity. I am so thankful for that, because I don't understand a lot of things happening right now. Why do some people suffer more than others? I don't get why I was born in the time and place I was. I don't understand why some people have more than I or why I have more than others. Help me remember there is a good and perfect eternal world that is my true home. When I feel anxious about what is happening here on earth, will You help me focus on Your promises for eternity? I may not understand everything that happens here, but I want to trust You at all times and with all my questions.

MAY 24

EPHESIANS 4:31

*Let all bitterness, anger and wrath,
shouting and slander be removed from you,
along with all malice.*

Father God, my anger doesn't have to turn into bitterness. But it's so easy to let that happen. I get angry over things that don't matter, then hold onto that anger. I let it grow and grow until it affects how I act toward other people. I hold grudges and talk behind people's backs. I complain about my family and the people who love me. Get rid of the bitterness in my heart, God! Take my anger and replace it with forgiveness and humility. Thank You for helping me let go of my anger before it turns into bitterness, and thank You for never being bitter toward me.

MAY 25

GALATIANS 5:16

I say, then, walk by the Spirit and you will certainly not carry out the desire of the flesh.

Holy Spirit, You have given me control over what I want! Sometimes I believe I have no control over my instincts. If I want something, I can't get it out of my head until I have it. But when my desires lead me to sin, I am never completely satisfied. I am always left wanting more. But the Bible says that if I am walking with You, I can tell those thoughts to be quiet. Please help me confess and turn away from any evil that is in my heart or mind. Help me live like You are walking beside me. I need You to direct my steps so that I honor You. Thank You so much for helping me fight against sin.

AMEN

MAY 26

PROVERBS 15:4

The tongue that heals is a tree of life, but a
devious tongue breaks the spirit.

Lord Jesus, You tell me to speak kind words to hurting people. Sometimes I feel awkward when people are upset. I don't know what to say. I am afraid I will say the wrong thing or make their pain worse. It's easier to walk away or move on than it is to say something encouraging. Give me the courage to speak kindness when I'm in situations that feel weird to me. Help me to say things that are uplifting and healing. Your kindness is overwhelming! You loved me so much that You died for me. You healed the sick and spent time with discouraged people. With Your help, I can show that same kindness to hurting people, too.

MAY 27

MATTHEW 15:8–9

"This people honors me with their lips, but their heart is far from me. They worship me in vain, teaching as doctrines human commands."

Father, it doesn't matter what my lips say if my heart isn't honoring You. It's so easy to say the right things at church without thinking about them. Sometimes I bow my head before a meal without being thankful. Or I raise my hands in worship all the while wondering what the other kids think of me. I even know how to give the right answer to my youth pastor to impress the adults around me. But none of those things matter if my heart isn't in the right place. Give me a heart that honors You—no matter what! Thank You for examining my heart and helping me see how it needs to change.

MAY 28

DEUTERONOMY 6:4–5

"Listen, Israel: The LORD our God, the LORD is one. Love the LORD your God with all your heart, with all your soul, and with all your strength."

God, I shouldn't love anything more than I love You. But I get distracted every single day. When I could be showing my love for You by reading the Bible, I usually scroll through my phone instead. I get distracted by texts when I'm praying. Sometimes my mind wanders off to what my friends are doing when I should be listening to my pastor at church. In my mind, I don't love anything more than You. So why do I let these distractions take my attention away from You? Will You help me love You so much that my first instinct is to put away anything that distracts me? I want to love You more than anyone or anything else on this earth. Thank You for loving me with a love that never fails.

MAY 29

JOHN 11:35

Jesus wept.

Jesus, every time I read this verse, I am amazed. You cried that Lazarus was dead, even though You knew You would raise Him from the dead soon. But You saw his sisters' pain and felt the weight of their sadness with them. Sometimes when my friends are in pain, it's easier to tell them it's all going to be okay than to sit with them in their sadness. Help me weep with those who weep—just like You did, Jesus. Thank You for sitting with me when I am sad. Help me to do the same for others.

MAY 30

PSALM 38:15

For I put my hope in you, LORD;
you will answer me, my Lord, my God.

God, You answer my prayers in Your timing, not mine. I don't always wait for You, though. I go to other people for advice or help. I am impatient. I want answers *now*, not later or when You say. Will You help me trust You instead of going to someone else? Help me to be content as I wait for You. You are making me more like You as I wait. I can always count on You to answer me, and I praise You for that. Thank You for not doing everything according to my timing, but answering when You know it's best.

MAY 31

PROVERBS 16:9

*A person's heart plans his way,
but the LORD determines his steps.*

Lord, I can ask for Your will to be done even when I don't understand it. It's really easy to get caught up in what I should be doing with my life. It feels like there is a blueprint for success. Any time something threatens that blueprint, I get anxious. I do everything I can to get the blueprint back on track instead of trusting You. Help me to ask You to guide me where I should go. Give me courage to pray boldly that You would do whatever is best, even if it goes against my best ideas. Thank You for always knowing what is best. Help me trust Your will!

NEW

JUNE 1

2 CORINTHIANS 10:5

*We take every thought
captive to obey Christ.*

God, You help me control my thoughts. It's hard to control my mind without You. My mind daydreams about what could be. Other times, it worries. Will I do well on a test? Should I tell my mom about my fight with my best friend? And sometimes I think about sin. I convince myself my sin is okay if I didn't mean to or if it didn't hurt anybody. Or—if I didn't *actually* sin, You don't *really* mind. But Your Word says to take my thoughts captive. Guide me to confess my thoughts and turn toward You. Help me take control of my sinful thoughts before they turn into sinful actions. Thank You for helping me and for always being with me.

JUNE 2

LUKE 9:61–62

Another said, "I will follow you, Lord, but first let me go and say good-bye to those at my house." But Jesus said to him, "No one who puts his hand to the plow and looks back is fit for the kingdom of God."

Father, even good things are not as valuable as You! Following You means I may have to leave some friendships behind. I might have to let go of my hopes and dreams. When I do, remind me that Your dreams are always so much better than anything I could imagine. Following You is better than everything! Help my love for You grow so much that even the best things—the *best* best friend, the nicest house—don't compare. I want to follow You wholeheartedly, no exceptions, and I want to do it for the rest of my life. There is nothing and no one on earth like You. Thank You for inviting me into Your family and giving me the strength to follow You, no matter what I have to leave behind.

JUNE 3

2 CORINTHIANS 1:3–4

Blessed be the God and Father of our Lord Jesus Christ, the Father of mercies and the God of all comfort. He comforts us in all our affliction, so that we may be able to comfort those who are in any kind of affliction, through the comfort we ourselves receive from God.

Lord Jesus, Your love—what comfort! Sometimes I feel like I am filled with sadness or fear. I get anxious about my future or worry my friends are leaving me out. It's like I am on the brink of exploding with emotion! I don't want to feel so tense, but I don't know how to stop. I need You to help me. Remind me how You comfort the hurting and anxious. You cried with Mary and Martha. You told Your disciple John to take care of Your mother. Please comfort me with the certainty that, even if things go wrong in my life, You are in control. I don't have to fight my anxious heart alone. Thank You for comforting me when everything inside me is raging.

JUNE 4

GALATIANS 1:10

*For am I now trying to persuade people,
or God? Or am I striving to please people?
If I were still trying to please people,
I would not be a servant of Christ.*

God, I don't have to strive to please others. But—I want to fit in. I feel like people are always looking at me and wondering why I am the way I am. When I speak against bullying or say I don't watch certain TV shows or follow celebrities online, people give me weird looks. It seems like my life would be easier if I just did what everyone else is doing. But You tell me to stand out for You. I want to resist being like everyone else and embrace looking just like Jesus. Help me to stop worrying about people accepting me. Guide me to follow You—no matter what anyone thinks. You served me with Your life! Now I want to live my life serving You.

NEW

JUNE 5

MATTHEW 23:28

"In the same way, on the outside you seem righteous to people, but inside you are full of hypocrisy and lawlessness."

Father God, only authentic faith pleases You. I am pretty good at showing off my faith for other people. I can give the right answers, pray a pretty good prayer in front of a group, and post the right Bible verses on social media. At times, I am a master at putting the best parts of my life on display and hiding the ugly parts—the sin, the worry, the fears. But I don't want to show off a fake faith, God. I want an *authentic* faith! I want to *want* You—and to realize how badly I *need* You. You see past my answers and showy prayers and Bible verses. You see inside my heart so make my faith genuine! Thank You for seeing the real me and for challenging me to follow You.

JUNE 6

REVELATION 22:13

*"I am the Alpha and the Omega, the first
and the last, the beginning and the end."*

Jesus Christ, You stay the same. No human can say that or do that. We all change. We will leave each other at some point—for school or work or some other reason. Some people will die before me, and I'll die before others. I won't be with this group of friends or my family forever. But You are the same. You have always been with me, and You will never leave me. Help me remember You are constant so I never trust anyone more than You. Thank You for always being with me—past, present, and future. You are the best friend I could ask for, Lord.

JUNE 7

1 PETER 4:10

*Just as each one has received a gift,
use it to serve others, as good stewards
of the varied grace of God.*

Jesus, thank You for coming to earth and showing me how to serve others. I confess I spend most of my time thinking about myself. It's easy to use my money and time on things that will make me happy. I rarely ask how I could help someone else. But when I read the Bible and see the way You lived Your life, I see how to put others first. You befriended anyone who came to You. You traveled from town to town, teaching people about Your love. Ultimately, You experienced a horrific death so that people like me could know and be loved by You. Lord, will You change my heart? I want to serve others, not myself. Thank You for serving me in Your life, death, and resurrection.

JUNE 8

EPHESIANS 4:26

Be angry and do not sin.
Don't let the sun go down on your anger.

God, You give me the strength to resist sin even when I am angry. It's hard! When I am mad at someone, I usually just let my emotions take over. I lash out or talk about that person to someone else. Anger leads me to do some terrible things. Will You help me control my anger before I sin? I want to have discipline when I'm mad, but I can only do that with Your help. Thank You for calming me when I feel rage and for being patient with me when I sin against You.

JUNE 9

MATTHEW 5:23–24

"So if you are offering your gift on the altar, and there you remember that your brother or sister has something against you, leave your gift there in front of the altar. First go and be reconciled with your brother or sister, and then come and offer your gift."

God, You care that I forgive people. But I sometimes tell myself other people don't deserve my forgiveness. If they did something bad enough, I hold a grudge. Other times I walk away from friends who hurt me or behave rudely toward them. But every time I don't forgive someone, I forget Your forgiveness. Thank You for valuing my relationships with other people. Help me to remember You forgave me when I didn't deserve it. Lead me in forgiving other people, too.

JUNE 10

REVELATION 22:20

He who testifies about these things says,
"Yes, I am coming soon."

Jesus, You are coming back! It's so easy to live my life as if this isn't true. I get wrapped up in my schedule and routine, as if this life is going to be my reality forever. I don't tell other people the good news: You came and died on the cross, and then You rose from the dead, promising to come back soon. I forget how urgent Your return is and stop inviting people to know You. Will You remind me to live like You are coming back today? Give me opportunities to have conversations about You. I want to share Your good news so the people in my life will be ready for You. Thank You for promising to return soon.

JUNE 11

1 TIMOTHY 6:6–7

But godliness with contentment is great gain.
For we brought nothing into the world,
and we can take nothing out.

Lord Jesus, I know that contentment honors You. When I hang out with people my age at school or church, sometimes all I see is what I don't have. I feel embarrassed if I don't have enough followers or the newest app or whatever everyone else is talking about. But even if I try, I'll never be able to keep up. Will You help me see You as my greatest treasure? Give me a heart that values what You value: Your people, Your Word, and You. I want to be content with what You give me. Thank You for Your promise that one day, I will have everything I need. I will be perfectly content in You.

JUNE 12

PROVERBS 19:17

Kindness to the poor is a loan to the LORD,
and he will give a reward to the lender.

Dear God, Christians are supposed to be known by their generosity to people in need. But I really struggle with selfishness—not just with money, but with my time, too. My heart doesn't care all that much about the needy people all around me. I tend to keep my money and time to myself so I will never be in need. But greed causes me to miss out on the joy found in generosity. Will You help me be generous with every gift You give me? Help me see everything I have as something I can give back to You. I want to trust You even when generosity doesn't make sense. Thank You for being the most generous being to ever exist. I want to be more like You in the way I give.

NEW

JUNE 13

Do you see a person who is wise in his own eyes?
There is more hope for a fool than for him.

Great God, my heart is so focused on how other people look at me! I want to always be right, sometimes so much that I throw everything I know in people's faces. I don't want to be looked down upon. But God, I don't always have to be right. I can't possibly know everything there is to know. I need to be humble, Lord, and I need to respect people instead of trying to prove how much I know. Give me a wise heart rather than one that assumes I know everything already. Thank You for holding all the wisdom and knowledge I need.

JUNE 14

PSALM 18:30

God—his way is perfect; the word of the LORD is pure. He is a shield to all who take refuge in him.

Father, Your way is best, even when I don't understand it. I admit I don't trust You very well, especially when I can't tell what You're doing. In my mind, I should be able to make sense of everything that happens to me. If something doesn't go my way, there must be a reason, right? Maybe there is, but that doesn't mean I need to know it. Help me trust You in every single circumstance, God! Remind me that Your way is the best way. You are a God who sees things I don't see. You keep me safe from things that could hurt me. Thank You for being trustworthy.

JUNE 15

1 PETER 2:24

*He himself bore our sins in his body
on the tree; so that, having died to sins,
we might live for righteousness.
By his wounds you have been healed.*

Jesus, my failures and flaws are no surprise to You. It's why You came to earth in the first place! Sometimes, though, I try to put on a good face. I hide my sin—as if You don't already know all about it! I feel embarrassed by the dark things in my heart, so I try to look like Your most faithful follower. But my darkness isn't a surprise to You, Lord. You came to earth to rescue me from it. I praise You for rescuing me. Thank You for seeing me, knowing me, and loving me, even though I am a sinner.

JUNE 16

PROVERBS 25:13

To those who send him, a trustworthy envoy is like the coolness of snow on a harvest day; he refreshes the life of his masters.

God, Your Word is like cold water on a hot day. When my friends come to me for advice, I usually tell them what I think they want to hear. Instead of telling them what I know they need, I try to make them happy. But Your Word gives life. I want to refresh my friends and family and everyone around me with Your words. Help me to encourage my friends with Your faithful and true Word. When people come to me for advice, I want to point to You before I point anywhere else. Thank You for using Your Word to recharge me when I need it. Help me share that refreshment with others.

NEW

JUNE 17

LUKE 4:43

*But he said to them, "It is necessary
for me to proclaim the good news about
the kingdom of God to the other towns also,
because I was sent for this purpose."*

Jesus, You give me strength to tell people about You! I admit I sometimes struggle to talk about You in my conversations. So many people I know and love don't believe in You and don't agree with Your teachings. If I mention You, I might make someone mad. That scares me, God. I hate it when people are upset with me, so I just avoid having those conversations. Will You give me confidence to share Your good news with friends and family who don't know You? I know they need You, and I want to tell them about You. Thank You for strengthening me to speak of You in my conversations!

JUNE 18

ISAIAH 26:3–4

*You will keep the mind that is dependent
on you in perfect peace,
for it is trusting in you.
Trust in the LORD forever,
because in the LORD, the LORD himself,
is an everlasting rock!*

God, Your Word tells me peace is worth more than my accomplishments. That truth clashes with what I hear. From what adults say about their jobs, it seems like my worth comes from how much I can achieve. Is that true, God? It sounds like a lot of pressure. But Your Word says to do something that doesn't make sense: slow down. It says my soul is more important than anything I can achieve. Help me know when I lose my way. Help me see when I am chasing accomplishments and achievements instead of You. Give me the ability to slow down and rest in Your love. Thank You for being my place of peace.

JUNE 19

1 CORINTHIANS 15:58

*Therefore, my dear brothers and sisters,
be steadfast, immovable, always excelling
in the Lord's work, because you know
that your labor in the Lord is not in vain.*

Father in heaven, I need to obey You with my whole heart. You see every part of my soul, so You know when I am not really following You. You see when I am embarrassed by my faith and avoid talking about You around my friends. I hate how often I pretend not to know You. I don't want to do that. Give me a heart so bursting with love for You that I can't help but tell everyone how good You are. Help me ask for Your wisdom before every decision I make and every word I say. Thank You for being worthy of all my love and obedience, Lord!

JUNE 20

PROVERBS 29:25

The fear of mankind is a snare,
but the one who trusts in the LORD is protected.

Dear Lord, You define who I am. I am Your beloved child! I don't need to seek affirmation from anyone else when I have You! In the past, I have longed for people to say how great I was. I wanted people to notice my hard work. I wanted them to see me as the best. Praise from people feels good! But chasing it is a trap. I have to keep chasing it. It never stops or lets up. But with You, I don't have to do anything. I am perfectly seen and loved by You. Help me remember Your affirmation is the most important. Thank You that I don't have to earn Your love!

NEW

JUNE 21

GENESIS 50:20

You planned evil against me; God planned it for good to bring about the present result.

God, You are working even when it looks like everything is falling apart. Sometimes it feels like nothing is going right—like I am messing everything up before it even happens. Will You show me You are working? You hold the future in Your hands even when I can't wrap my mind around what is coming next. Help me remember You are good, and You do good. When it looks like things are coming apart, You are putting something together. Thank You for always working in my life.

JUNE 22

GALATIANS 5:24

Now those who belong to Christ Jesus have crucified the flesh with its passions and desires.

Holy Spirit, my desires aren't in control anymore! I have sometimes acted like I don't have any choice in my sin. If my mind decides it wants to do something badly enough, I can't help but do it. That was true *before* I knew You. But now that Jesus is Lord of my life, and now that You live in me, I do have control. You help me listen and obey Your teaching. I can stop myself from going down a wrong path. Help me resist sin! Make me someone who follows You instead of my desires. Thank You for working in my heart every day so I can be more obedient to You!

JUNE 23

JOHN 15:5

"I am the vine; you are the branches. The one who remains in me and I in him produces much fruit, because you can do nothing without me."

Jesus, when I depend on You wholly, I grow in ways I never imagined. Sometimes when I look at other Christians, I wonder if I will ever get to where they are. Will I ever stop thinking of myself first? Will I ever love reading the Bible as much as they do? Will I ever pray out loud without having to work out my words in advance? I know I can't grow into a mature Christian on my own. I need Your help, Lord. Your Word promises that if I rely on You like a branch relies on its vine, You will help me grow. I want to grow, Jesus! I want to become more like You. Thank You for producing good fruits like patience, love, and joy in me when I remain in You.

JUNE 24

2 CORINTHIANS 5:20

Therefore, we are ambassadors for Christ, since God is making his appeal through us. We plead on Christ's behalf, "Be reconciled to God."

Jesus, I get really concerned about what other people think of me. I worry they won't be impressed by my clothes or my grades or my friends. I let what others think of me determine how I act and what I do. It's exhausting. Will You help me stop caring so much about people's opinions and start caring about how I represent You? Your Word says that I am an ambassador! When I reflect Your character and share the gospel, people can come to know You as God. I want how I represent You to be the only thing I am concerned about. Thank You for shining through me, Jesus!

JUNE 25

LUKE 5:16

Yet he often withdrew to deserted places and prayed.

Christ Jesus, my relationship with You isn't for show. I know I shouldn't care what other people think about my personal relationship with You, but sometimes, it's all I can think about. When I am around other Christians, I want to show off how much I know about You or how much I love You. Will You help me live more like You did? You went away to pray. You weren't putting on a show; You cared about Your relationship with Your Father. If anyone deserves to show off, it is You! Help me seek You in private before I do anything publicly. Thank You for showing me how to follow and love You, Jesus.

JUNE 26

PROVERBS 1:20–21

*Wisdom calls out in the street; she makes
her voice heard in the public squares.
She cries out above the commotion;
she speaks at the entrance of the city gates.*

Father God, You freely give wisdom to those who trust You. How amazing is that?! Sometimes, I feel like such a baby Christian. I should come to You in prayer more often or understand my Bible better by now. I should always trust You. But I'm not there yet. With Your help, though, I *can* develop wisdom. I want to be someone who reads Your Word and understands what You're saying. I want to remember to pray more and trust You in every circumstance of my life. Will You make me a wise person? Thank You for helping me grow in wisdom every day!

JUNE 27

ECCLESIASTES 11:5

Just as you don't know the path of the wind, or how bones develop in the womb of a pregnant woman, so also you don't know the work of God who makes everything.

Father God, Your mysteries make me want to know You more. I have a lot of questions about how things work in this world. I don't understand how You created everything with words. I don't understand how or why the universe works the way it does. I don't even understand how my mind is able to look at the words on this page and make sense of them. But You do, God! You created all that exists, and You know the answer behind every single mystery I don't understand. Help me trust You as the God who holds the answer to every mystery.

JUNE 28

DEUTERONOMY 31:6

*"Be strong and courageous; don't be terrified
or afraid of them. For the LORD your God
is the one who will go with you; he will
not leave you or abandon you."*

Lord, when I am afraid, I can turn to You. The future is scary. I think a lot about who *won't* be in my future. Will I lose my family? Who will my friends be? Will I get to have a family of my own, or will I be alone? Is life going to get better? Or will it get worse? When questions like this race around in my mind, will You help me look to You? No matter what the future holds, You will be there. You will hold me through every turn my life takes. Thank You that You are the answer to all my questions, and thank You that I don't have to be afraid. You are *always* with me!

JUNE 29

2 TIMOTHY 2:16

*Avoid irreverent and empty speech,
since those who engage in it will
produce even more godlessness.*

God, gossip is not of You. It can be really hard to walk away when people are talking about others. It's such a normal part of life that I don't always realize it's happening until I have already joined in. But I don't want to be a part of something that dishonors You. Will You make me someone who recognizes gossip and stops it in its tracks? Help me to be a Christian who cares deeply about other people. I want to reflect Your love for others in the way I use my words. Thank You for Your love for people, and thank You for caring about how I love people, too.

JUNE 30

2 TIMOTHY 4:7

I have fought the good fight, I have finished the race, I have kept the faith.

Father in heaven, holding onto my faith is a worthwhile fight. Sometimes I get lazy or tired, though. I start living like the rest of the world. The Bible tells me holding onto my faith will take effort. It is a race for all of life. But some of my friends say I don't have to do anything if it makes me uncomfortable. Will You help me reject that idea? I know that keeping my faith when everyone around me tells me to give it up will be worth it. At the end of my life, I'll get the ultimate prize: life forever with You.

JULY 1

Now may the God of hope fill you with all joy and peace as you believe so that you may overflow with hope by the power of the Holy Spirit.

Holy Spirit, You help me choose faith over fear! When I live in fear, I can't help but imagine every single, horrible situation. I start to believe my life will be a series of worst-case scenarios, and I freeze. I can't move. I am scared something terrifying will happen. But You promise that even in the face of the scariest circumstance, even if someone I love dies or my plans for the future collapse, I can have joy! I can even have peace. Give me faith in You when peace seems impossible and joy unreachable. I want to overflow with hope because You are with me. You guide me and help me reject fear and hold tight to faith. Thank You for filling me with Your power!

JULY 2

EXODUS 17:12

When Moses's hands grew heavy, they took a stone and put it under him, and he sat down on it. Then Aaron and Hur supported his hands, one on one side and one on the other so that his hands remained steady until the sun went down.

Father in heaven, You give me friends to help me when I am weak. It's so hard to admit my weaknesses to other Christians. What will they think of me? Will they still want me around if they know my flaws? Sometimes it's easier to pretend I am not struggling at all. But when I look to Your Word, I see that even Moses needed help from people around him. He needed his brother and friend to hold his hands up. Will You help me admit my weakness to other Christians so they can help me? Give me Christian friends to hold me up when I'm weak. Help me hold them up, too!

JULY 3

PROVERBS 24:16

Though a righteous person falls seven times, he will get up, but the wicked will stumble into ruin.

God, even when I fail, You let me return to You. I know what is right and wrong, but I still choose sin. I fail over and over again, and I feel embarrassed to come to You. I know I chose my way instead of Yours. But You don't shame me, God. When I fall into sin, You just ask me to get up and return to You. Will You help me move past my embarrassment so I can be comforted by You? Help me to stop stumbling and falling into sin, and help me to be confident in Your grace and mercy. Thank You for forgiving me and welcoming me when I choose sin.

JULY 4

"Master," Simon replied, "we've worked hard all night long and caught nothing. But if you say so, I'll let down the nets."

Jesus, Your way doesn't always make sense. When You ask me to do something I don't understand, some of my friends tell me to forget about You. They say I should just follow my heart. But I know that even when Your directions don't make sense to anyone else, You are working in ways I can't see. Will You give me the determination to follow You in every circumstance? I want to choose You, no matter who is looking or what they think about me. Thank You for always being trustworthy, even when I can't see what You're doing.

JULY 5

ISAIAH 61:10

*I rejoice greatly in the LORD, I exult in my God;
for he has clothed me with the garments
of salvation and wrapped me in a robe of
righteousness, as a groom wears a turban
and as a bride adorns herself with her jewels.*

Lord of salvation, I praise You for giving me new life! Sometimes I find myself more excited by things in this world than I am about salvation. I spend so much time dressing for other people's approval or buying things that will impress my friends. I forget I already have what matters most: Your saving grace! Your Word says I should rejoice that You have saved me from my sin, not in my status with my friends or in what I own. Help me value salvation as the most precious thing I have—because it is! Give me a heart that doesn't take Your salvation for granted.

JULY 6

LUKE 12:28

If that's how God clothes the grass, which is in the field today and is thrown into the furnace tomorrow, how much more will he do for you—you of little faith?

Father God, You provide everything I need! But if I'm not careful, I stop believing You'll provide for me. I start to believe I can take care of myself. If I work hard enough, if I make the smartest moves, if I get into the right school or get the right job, then maybe I can make it on my own. But trying to care for all my needs without coming to You for help only leaves me anxious and worried. I need reminders that You are the one who provides. Give me a heart that trusts You. Thank You for always giving me everything I need in life to be a faithful follower of You!

NEW

JULY 7

ROMANS 12:4–5

"Now as we have many parts in one body, and all the parts do not have the same function, in the same way we who are many are one body in Christ and individually members of one another."

King Jesus, You use so many kinds of people in Your plans! I usually see differences as bad. I tend to hang out with people who are like me. I get nervous when I have to spend time with people who *aren't* like me. But Your Word teaches that You use all our different gifts and abilities for Your glory! On our own, none of us can reflect You fully, but together, we get a little closer. People of different races, ages, genders, and nations are part of Your family and Your plan! Help me see the value in difference just like You do, and help me seek out friends who are different from me. Thank You for making us all different. It is for my good and Your glory!

JULY 8

1 Corinthians 2:16

For who has known the Lord's mind, that he may instruct him? But we have the mind of Christ.

Jesus, thank You for giving me Your mind through the Holy Spirit! Sometimes I wonder how You lived in the same world I live in and *never* sinned. Your mind didn't wander into disobedience like mine does. When I am going about my life—going to school or the library or the movies—I see opportunities to sin everywhere. If I know something will bring me temporary happiness, I can't get it out of my head. I have a really hard time saying "no." But when You gave me the Holy Spirit, You gave me the ability to have Your mind—Your mind that chose to turn away from sin every single time it was in front of You. Will You help me choose to do the same thing? Thank You for giving me the ability to say "no" to sin through Your power!

JULY 9

2 CORINTHIANS 8:13–14

It is not that there should be relief for others and hardship for you, but it is a question of equality. At the present time your surplus is available for their need, so that their abundance may in turn meet your need, in order that there may be equality.

God, You call Christians to use our money to help people in need. Right now, I don't own a lot. Even if I give 10 percent of all the money I make, it's not that much. Am I even making a difference? Will I have enough left over for the things I need? Please help me choose generosity. I want to be obedient to Your call to share what I have, not grudgingly, but out of love. Help me see every penny You give me as an opportunity to pass a gift on to others. Thank You for being so generous to me, God! I don't deserve Your blessings, but I am so thankful for them.

JULY 10

EXODUS 33:14

*And he [LORD] replied, "My presence will
go with you, and I will give you rest."*

Lord, I don't have to earn my rest in You. I tend to believe that if I can just please You enough, then You will give me peace. If I can just follow You closely enough, then You will take away my worries. Will You remind me that You don't make me work to earn time or rest with You? Even my best efforts could never earn Your love, because You give it to me freely. Help me rest with You today, Jesus! Thank You for being with me, wherever I go and whatever I do.

JULY 11

1 CORINTHIANS 11:1

Imitate me, as I also imitate Christ.

Father God, You have put so many people in my life who show me what it looks like to pursue You completely! I want to imitate them. Their faith in You is incredible and such an encouragement. But God, it's so easy to look at people who live for human approval and think they have it all put together. They might claim You as God, but their relationships with You don't go deep. I don't want to follow their example. I don't want to settle for a lifeless relationship with You. I want real life and real relationship and be the best follower of You I can be. Help me imitate the people who love You with their whole hearts.

JULY 12

HEBREWS 4:12

*For the word of God is living and effective
and sharper than any double-edged sword,
penetrating as far as the separation of soul and
spirit, joints and marrow. It is able to judge the
thoughts and intentions of the heart.*

Lord, Your Word is life-changing! Making time to read the Bible every day is hard. I typically prioritize other things, from unimportant things like social media and my appearance to important things like schoolwork and relationships with my family and friends. I always have something that seems like a bigger priority than Your Word. But when I spend time with You by reading Your Word, everything in my life takes on new meaning. I see social media and appearances for what they are—completely temporary—and I approach things like schoolwork and relationships through the lens of Your love. Help me to prioritize reading Your Word so my life looks more and more like Yours. I want everyone to see how I've been changed by You! Thank You for giving me Your Word, the Bible.

JULY 13

MATTHEW 5:16

"In the same way, let your light shine before others, so that they may see your good works and give glory to your Father in heaven."

Jesus, thank You for teaching me that good works honor God and lead people to praise Him. Sometimes it seems like serving others or being nice to them is something I should do for myself. If I'm kind to people, maybe they'll be kind to me, too. When I get on someone's good side, maybe they will do something good for me in exchange. I know my heart isn't where it needs to be when I only think about myself. Will You help me practice kindness, not to get something out of it, but so that people will know You? Thank You for reminding me how to love people best. I want to glorify You in everything I say and do.

JULY 14

PSALM 18:6

I called to the LORD in my distress, and I cried to my God for help. From his temple he heard my voice, and my cry to him reached his ears.

God, You always hear me when I cry out to You. Sometimes I wonder if You think my cries are annoying. I know You see all the horrible things happening on the earth—war, homelessness, disease, and hunger. How can what I am going through *really* matter to You? My issues aren't that big of a deal. How could You care about them, with everything else going on in the world? When I feel this way, I tend to cover up my sadness. I pretend I'm fine and don't cry out to You for help. Will You help me stop believing those lies? You always hear me when I am in distress, no matter how big or small it is. Thank You for hearing and caring for me, God.

JULY 15

1 JOHN 2:15

Do not love the world or the things in the world. If anyone loves the world, the love of the Father is not in him.

Father, when I focus on earthly possessions—my next phone or jacket or book or even favorite snacks—my love for You diminishes. It's so hard to not want what everyone else has. Sometimes, when I spend time with my friends, I become jealous of them. Why do some people have more than others? Sometimes I want to be just like them and have what they have. Will You replace my love for things with love for You? Help me to stop seeing all the things I don't have, and to start thanking You for what I do have, including my relationship with You! I know Your love is worth more than anything I could ever own, and it will last forever. Help me focus on Your never-ending love. Thank You for loving me!

JULY 16

GALATIANS 6:9

Let us not get tired of doing good, for we will reap at the proper time if we don't give up.

God in heaven, You help me follow You even when I am tired. If I'm being honest, sometimes I don't want to follow You. It is exhausting to constantly say "no" to things I want to do. Fighting against sin is tiring—especially when it seems like no one else wants to follow You. But Your Word promises that, even if I can't see it now, I will be rewarded for following You. That reward might not look like popularity or possessions or anything else in this world, but I trust You. Your reward is always better. Help me obey You, planting seeds now that can be harvested in the future. Thank You for how You work in my life!

JULY 17

PSALM 103:17

But from eternity to eternity the LORD's faithful love is toward those who fear him, and his righteousness toward the grandchildren.

Lord, I feel like I constantly work for people's approval and love. I want to please everyone. I think if I make them happy, I can earn their love. But what if their love runs out? I am scared to let people down. Maybe they will stop loving me. But God, this verse reminds me that Your love for me never runs out! Even if I sin, even if I mess up, Your love for me is constant. You loved me before I was even born. Nothing I do can make You approve of me or love me more. Will You help me believe that? When I am tempted to look for perfect love in people, help me look to You instead. Thank You so much for Your everlasting love!

JULY 18

PHILIPPIANS 4:11

I don't say this out of need, for I have learned to be content in whatever circumstances I find myself.

Father, when I am content in You, I find peace. The world tells me to find my own peace—if I do what makes me happy, I will be content. But the things that make me happy don't always leave me content. Most of the time, they leave me wanting more. Help me trust You for abundant peace, God. Help me follow You instead of chasing after the things that I think will make me happy. I know You are the only one who can bring true contentment to my heart. Thank You for being everything I need, and thank You for giving me peace when I trust in You.

JULY 19

PROVERBS 27:17

Iron sharpens iron,
and one person sharpens another.

Lord, I need Your help in choosing my closest friends. Most of the time, I tend to choose people who don't challenge me to be more like Jesus. I am not thinking like You when I decide who I want to be friends with. I get blinded by popularity and status. Before I know it, I am trying to look more like my friends than You. Will You help me form friendships with people who are trying to follow You? I know I should be friends with people who don't know You so I can tell them about You. But I want my very closest friends to be sisters and brothers in Christ who encourage me to look more like Him. Thank You for always being with me and guiding me toward friendships that please You.

JULY 20

MATTHEW 17:20

"Because of your little faith," he told them. "For truly I tell you, if you have faith the size of a mustard seed, you will tell this mountain, 'Move from here to there,' and it will move. Nothing will be impossible for you."

Jesus, the world tells me that if I just believe in myself, I can do the impossible. But that's not true. I have believed in myself plenty of times and still failed. And, even if I reach the highest levels of success or accomplish amazing things, they would mean nothing without You. You say You work miracles through faith—but not faith in *myself*, faith in *You*. Will You help me look to You when I am doing something that feels impossible? Will You do things through me so anyone watching is pointed to You? I love You, Lord! Give me faith the size of a mustard seed, and grow it into something even bigger.

JULY 21

2 TIMOTHY 1:7

For God has not given us a spirit of fear,
but one of power, love, and sound judgment.

God, Your Word reminds me I don't have to be controlled by fear. When fear and anxiety come over me, they rule my whole day. They affect the way I talk to people and how much I get done. I just can't seem to shake the anxiety and nervousness. On days when I am fearful, I need Your power, love, and sound judgment. Through Your Holy Spirit, I can remember You are good even when everything looks bad. It's only through Your power that I can overcome fear and trust You are in control. Thank You so much for Your love. It sets me free from crippling fear!

JULY 22

2 TIMOTHY 3:16

*All Scripture is inspired by God and
is profitable for teaching, for rebuking, for
correcting, for training in righteousness.*

Father, I can trust every word in the Bible! I have heard people say the Bible isn't trustworthy. Or they say it's irrelevant. It is too old to apply to my life. Sometimes I am tempted to believe what they say, especially when the Bible is confusing or hard to understand. When that happens, I just want to give up and pretend Your Word does not matter. But every single word in the Bible matters! You inspired all of it, and I can trust all of it! Will You help me remember there is no limit to Your wisdom? Your wisdom lasts forever. Help me read the Bible—the parts I understand and the parts I don't—with a heart that wants to know You more. Thank You for every word of Scripture!

JULY 23

2 CORINTHIANS 9:7

Each person should do as he has decided in his heart—not reluctantly or out of compulsion, since God loves a cheerful giver.

Dear Jesus, when I help other people, I should do it joyfully! Without Your help, I tend to be a selfish person. I am a reluctant giver, not a cheerful one. Giving up my time, money, or energy feels like a burden. But You call me to be cheerful in my giving! I need Your help to do that. Help me move from selfishness to generosity. Thank You for being the ultimate giver! You are more generous than I could ever hope to be. You left heaven for earth, You served everyone You met, and You laid down Your life for sinners. Help me look more like You as I give my time and money to others.

JULY 24

MARK 14:41

Then he [Jesus] came a third time and said to them, "Are you still sleeping and resting? Enough! The time has come. See, the Son of Man is betrayed into the hands of sinners."

Jesus, You experienced every part of being a human, including loneliness. My heart definitely feels lonely sometimes. Following Your Word and Your ways isn't easy—especially when people around me don't. Sometimes I just want to give up! But thank You for reminding me that You are fully human and fully God. You know what it feels like to stand up for the truth, even when You were the only one doing it. Will You help me look to You as my example when I am the only one trying to follow You? Thank You, Lord, for understanding me with all my weaknesses and for using them to encourage me to depend more on You.

JULY 25

JOHN 16:33

"I have told you these things so that in me you may have peace. You will have suffering in this world. Be courageous! I have conquered the world."

Lord, You never change. You are the same when life is easy and when life is hard. Sometimes I believe trusting in You means things should go well for me. If I have You on my side, shouldn't I be successful? Shouldn't I have the friends, relationships, schools, and jobs I want? But Your Word doesn't promise my life will be easy because I know You. It actually promises I will experience hard things. Will You help me trust You when things are difficult and when they are easy? Remind me that You are with me in every situation I face, and every single situation—even the hard ones—is from You.

JULY 26

SONG OF SONGS 2:7

*I charge you by the gazelles and the wild
does of the field, do not stir up or awaken
love until the appropriate time.*

Lord, You created sex for marriage. But culture says I should be doing it now—that it doesn't matter if I am married or not. I know some of my friends are having sex now, so why should I wait? You promise there is a blessing in having sex in the right context. Will You help me wait for marriage? Even when it feels impossible, will You give me the strength to wait that I don't have on my own? Thank You for the gift of physical intimacy. Give me a heart that values obeying You more than giving in to my desires.

JULY 27

JEREMIAH 31:25

*For I satisfy the thirsty person and feed
all those who are weak.*

Father, it seems like depression is all around me. If I am not struggling with it, I know someone who is. This world is filled with things to be sad about too—sickness, death, abuse, oppression, poverty—the list goes on and on. When I think about all that's wrong with the world, I sometimes feel hopeless. But when I am weary, sad, and weak, You are strong. You give me Your strength. Help me remember You are bigger than all that is wrong in this world. One day, You will make a world free of abuse, poverty, oppression, and even death! Thank You for strengthening me with Your power. When the world leaves me sad and empty, You leave me satisfied and full.

JULY 28

They said to each other, "Weren't our hearts burning within us while he was talking with us on the road and explaining the Scriptures to us?"

God, Your truth ignites my heart with love for You! No matter how hard I try, I can't make myself love You on my own. Even if it looks like I am following Your commands to the letter, if I am obeying You without loving You, what is the point? If I am only trying to love You with my actions, it's like putting gasoline on wood and expecting it to catch fire. Just like the men on the road to Emmaus, I need Your help understanding Scripture. I need You to give me a passion for Your truth. Please be my flame! Help me follow You, not because I want to be a better person, but because You have made my heart burn with love for You! Thank You for setting my heart on fire.

JULY 29

JAMES 3:2

For we all stumble in many ways. If anyone does not stumble in what he says, he is mature, able also to control the whole body.

Jesus, You are bigger than my mistakes! I have made mistakes that have led to a lot of pain, especially with the words I say. Some of my words have cost me friendships or my family's trust. When I mess up, I wonder if You can still use someone like me. I cause people so much pain sometimes! Your Word is so encouraging to me in those moments. Will You remind me that even if I mess up, You can use my mistakes for Your plans? Help me depend on You when I succeed and say kind words, and when I fail and say hurtful ones.

JULY 30

JOHN 1:5

That light shines in the darkness, and yet the darkness did not overcome it.

Jesus, Your light is so bright that all the darkness in the world cannot overpower it! Without You, I would be without hope, stuck in my sin and deserving of death. But You are light! You brought hope to a dark and defeated world. You brought hope to my life, too, by dying in my place and taking my punishment for sin. The darkness was no match for You, Jesus! I can't wait for the day when sin will be defeated forever, and I can live in eternity with You. Help me focus on Your light when the world is dark. I love You, Lord.

NEW

JULY 31

1 CORINTHIANS 6:19–20

Don't you know that your body is a temple of the Holy Spirit who is in you, whom you have from God? You are not your own, for you were bought at a price. So glorify God with your body.

Father God, thank You that my body is important to You. It's easy to believe that what I do with my body doesn't matter since it doesn't really affect anyone else. But You care about my body so much that You sent Your Spirit to live in me. Will You help me treat my body as a temple? Help me value this body You have given me as much as You do, and help me know when I am sinning with my body. I want to follow You with my spiritual self and my physical self. Thank You for caring about every single part of me, Lord!

AUGUST 1

Those who look to him are radiant with joy;
their faces will never be ashamed.

God, in your presence, joy always outweighs shame. I admit I sometimes feel weighed down by my past. When I think about decisions I have made, shame creeps into my heart and makes me hot with embarrassment. But when I look to You, I'm reminded You see Jesus's righteousness. That makes me so happy, God! Help me come to You when I feel ashamed of my past, and give me joy in the truth that You love me despite every wrong thing I have done. Thank You for calling me to stop fixating on my past and to start being radiant with joy by looking at You!

AUGUST 2

COLOSSIANS 1:17

*He is before all things, and by him
all things hold together.*

Jesus, You hold everything in the world together. But I sometimes fear every good thing in my life is going to shatter into a billion tiny pieces. And, when things seem to be going exceptionally well, it's like a little voice in my head won't stop talking. It tells me none of it will last. Every good thing is too good to be true. But Jesus, Your Word says that even before anything was created, You were holding everything together. You are both too good to be true *and* true! Remind me of that when things are falling apart. Help me know You are holding me. Thank You for being completely in control of everything.

AUGUST 3

ROMANS 8:28

We know that all things work together
for the good of those who love God,
who are called according to his purpose.

Father in heaven, You are trustworthy, even when I experience the worst thing I could possibly imagine. When I think about losing the people I am closest to—I am terrified. I can't imagine life without my family or friends, and I don't really want to. But God, this world is broken. My relationships, as good as they are, might not last as long as I want them to. Will You help me trust You with the scariest thing I could imagine? I want the knowledge of Your goodness to apply to my best days and my worst fears. Help me to love You and trust You, no matter what I face.

AUGUST 4

1 THESSALONIANS 5:14

*And we exhort you, brothers and sisters:
warn those who are idle, comfort the discouraged,
help the weak, be patient with everyone.*

Lord, You call me to be patient with people, even the people who are hard to love. When someone I know always complains or seems constantly sad, I want to walk away. I don't like being around negative people, and I get annoyed with people who can't see the good around them. I need patience that comes from You, God. I know that negative people probably need encouragement, because when I am feeling down, I need encouragement. I want to be a comforter and encourager who points people to You. Thank You for being patient with me, especially when I am hard to love. Please help me do the same thing for others.

LUKE 6:28

*"Bless those who curse you,
pray for those who mistreat you."*

Father God, when I am bullied, help me to respond with kindness instead of hate. In a world where people can be mean and hide behind a screen, it seems like hatred is everywhere. Whether it's people bullying me or someone else, I want to speak up, but I want to do it in a way that glorifies You. Will You help me respond to unkind people with love? I want You to change the hearts of the bullies I encounter, and I want to be a part of that process. Thank You for using me to show people Your love!

AUGUST 6

PSALM 100:2

Serve the LORD with gladness;
come before him with joyful songs.

Jesus, so much joy is found in serving You! Sometimes serving You feels like just another thing I *should* be doing. When I think like that—adding it to my list of responsibilities—I get tired. It's another box to check off. But Your Word reminds me service is not about checking off a box. It's about joy! I need my heart to be changed. I need Your Spirit to give me the passion to follow You. I can't create it on my own. I want everything I say and do to be out of excitement to serve You. Thank You for being a God of joy!

AUGUST 7

MARK 14:34

He said to them, "I am deeply grieved to the point of death. Remain here and stay awake."

Jesus, You felt every single emotion I could feel. Sometimes I wonder how, if You knew everything—if You knew the happy ending of Your story, that You would rise from the dead and defeat sin, death, and Satan forever—how could You ever really be sad? Remind me what You told Your disciples in this verse. You felt all the pain and grief that I feel, and You are with me as I grieve, too. Comfort me in my sadness and show me how I can glorify You with every single emotion—just like You glorified God in everything You felt. Thank You for coming to earth and living a human life with human emotions. I am so grateful that You understand my feelings.

NEW

AUGUST 8

MATTHEW 24:14

"This good news of the kingdom will be proclaimed in all the world as a testimony to all nations, and then the end will come."

God, You call me to share the good news of Jesus as if I don't have any time left on earth. I so easily go through my routines and life without ever talking about You with my friends and family. I am so busy with everything I have on my plate: school and chores and siblings. On top of that, I usually spend my free time doing mindless things so I can have a break. But none of those things are eternal, God. Help me spend my free time looking for ways I can share the gospel with people around me. I want to shout Your good news in every sliver of free time I have. Give me gospel opportunities every day, God, and convict my heart when I choose to stay quiet. Thank You for giving me the opportunity to share Your good news with others!

AUGUST 9

PSALM 121:7

*The LORD will protect you from
all harm; he will protect your life.*

Lord, You protect me from harm. Sometimes I am afraid to ask for Your protection. I worry that hardship or sadness might mean You have let me down or You didn't hear my prayer. But Your Word tells me that's not true. You won't allow me to fall outside of Your protection. No matter what hardships I experience, help me to remember You are my faithful protector. You never let me down, and You always hear my prayers! Thank You for keeping me safe. Thank You for protecting my life.

AMEN

AUGUST 10

1 THESSALONIANS 3:5

For this reason, when I could no longer stand it, I also sent him to find out about your faith, fearing that the tempter had tempted you and that our labor might be for nothing.

King of heaven, I can stand firm in You when I am tempted to sin! Sometimes I feel completely powerless when I face temptation. If other people are sinning around me, how can I say "no"? How will I stand the embarrassment of sticking out? It's easier to just give in to temptation and then come to You for forgiveness later. But that is not how You want me to live! I need Your help to stand firm and resist sin. I know I can do this because You have given me Your power through the Holy Spirit. Thank You for giving me the power to take a stand against sin!

AUGUST 11

PROVERBS 12:15

A fool's way is right in his own eyes,
but whoever listens to counsel is wise.

God, sound advice is something I should pay attention to. But it's hard to hear Your wisdom. All kinds of messages beg for my attention, telling me what to buy, how to look, what to listen to and watch, and how popular I should be. It's so easy to listen to those messages, even if they don't lead me to follow You. Will You help me know what advice is good and wise and what advice is not? I want to pay closer attention when You put people in my life who lead me to follow You. Thank You for giving me wise counsel and convicting me to listen to it.

NEW

AUGUST 12

REVELATION 5:9

And they sang a new song:
You are worthy to take the scroll
and to open its seals,
because you were slaughtered,
and you purchased a people
for God by your blood
from every tribe and language
and people and nation.

Lord, Your Word reminds me that Your kingdom will be filled with people from every tribe, tongue, and nation. You say heaven will be filled with lots of people: people who are like me and people who aren't. It's so easy to be friends with people who are like me, but I want to get out of my comfort zone and start spending time with people different from me. I want my life here on earth to look a little more like heaven. That means making friends with people who look different from me or who like different foods or who have different family traditions. Thank You that Your salvation isn't for one kind of person. It's for everyone!

AUGUST 13

EPHESIANS 6:18

Pray at all times in the Spirit with every prayer and request, and stay alert with all perseverance and intercession for all the saints.

Father God, You want my life to be full of prayer! I spend so much time running all my ideas by the people who know me best. I share my thoughts and process the things I am confused about with my friends and family. I talk to people about what excites me and what scares me. So why do I forget to talk to You? Please make me into a person who never stops talking with You. I want my thoughts to be constant prayer, thanking You for every joy I experience and crying out to You every time I am afraid. Thank You for always hearing me when I pray, and for helping me come to You when I need guidance!

AUGUST 14

PROVERBS 20:19

The one who reveals secrets is a constant gossip; avoid someone with a big mouth.

Dear Jesus, gossip shouldn't be part of my friendships, yet I often fall into gossip's trap. It usually starts with a normal, innocent conversation, but if I don't pay attention, my friends and I end up talking about someone else in a way that doesn't honor You. I want a heart that recognizes gossip before it leaves my mouth—that sees it coming before I even start talking. Will You give that to me? Give me a heart that is pure. Help me think about You before I open my mouth to gossip about anyone else. Thank You for convicting me when I sin, and thank You for holding me accountable to loving other people as You would.

AUGUST 15

COLOSSIANS 3:2

*Set your minds on things above,
not on earthly things.*

Lord, You give me the power to set my mind on godly things. Every morning, I think this will be the day I focus only on You. I have every intention to pray more, to read the Bible more, and even to talk more about You with my friends and family. Then I get distracted. I see something that captures my thoughts, or I get angry because of something someone did. I need You to remind me that I *can* set my mind on You again, even if I do get distracted throughout the day. Will You encourage me to keep thinking about God? Encourage me to pray when I am angry, to read the Bible when I am having sinful thoughts, and to share all the good things You are doing in my life with my family and friends. Thank You for helping me set my mind on godly things!

AUGUST 16

PSALM 147:3

*He heals the brokenhearted
and bandages their wounds.*

Father God, I can trust You to heal my broken heart. Sometimes I feel completely overwhelmed with sadness. My friends let me down and break my heart over and over again. I know I probably have crazy-high expectations for my friends and my family. When they don't meet my expectations, I feel let down and unloved. But God, I can't expect any one person to meet *all* my expectations, and I know that people can never be the source of my happiness. Help me let go of any unrealistic expectations I have so I can love my friends and family better. Help me trust You for all my needs. Thank You for being someone who exceeds all my expectations and heals my heart when I am feeling down.

AUGUST 17

1 Timothy 4:12

Don't let anyone despise your youth,
but set an example for the believers in speech,
in conduct, in love, in faith, and in purity.

Lord, my age doesn't make me incapable of big faith! When I see adults doing amazing things for the gospel, I wonder why I bother. Am I even making that big of a difference? I wonder if people will take me and my faith seriously, or if everyone knows I am too young to *really* follow You. Will You help me overcome my doubts? Help me to trust You and to have faith in You, no matter what age I am. Your Word says You work through even young people like me. Thank You for using me to spread the gospel and even allowing me to set an example for other people.

AUGUST 18

COLOSSIANS 3:12

*Therefore, as God's chosen ones, holy
and dearly loved, put on compassion,
kindness, humility, gentleness, and patience.*

Jesus, I want my friendships to be marked by compassion, kindness, humility, gentleness, and patience. But Jesus, too often even my Christian friendships look like the world's. We are quick to gossip, we leave other people out, we are impatient with one another, and we do so many other sinful things. Will You help us put away our sinful habits and start living like we've been changed by the Holy Spirit? I want people to look at my friendships and see relationships that honor You. I want to be known for treating other people with dignity and kindness. Help me be compassionate, kind, humble, gentle, and patient with everyone around me. Thank You for being all those things with me! I love You, Lord.

AUGUST 19

JEREMIAH 17:9

*The heart is more deceitful than anything else,
and incurable—who can understand it?*

Jesus, most of the time, I would rather follow my heart than follow You. I convince myself that my heart will lead me to true happiness and if I feel lost, my heart will save me. But Lord, my heart deceives me. It often leads me somewhere I don't want to go. It tells me to put myself first, and it regularly catches me in a web of conflict and lies. If I listen to my heart, it eventually shows just how sinful I really am. Help me chase after You instead of my heart, Jesus. Give me the strength to say "no" to my deceitful heart and "yes" to You. Thank You for being better than every desire of my heart!

AUGUST 20

PHILIPPIANS 4:13

*I am able to do all things through
him who strengthens me.*

God in heaven, thank You for reminding me that I can get through any hard circumstance with Your strength. When I was younger, I believed with all my heart that nothing was impossible. I felt I could be anything I wanted to be—a hero, a dancer, an astronaut, even royalty. But now that I am older, it sometimes feels like nothing is possible. I find myself struggling with anxiety and depression, and I don't think I can ever escape those feelings. Will You remind me that it is not my strength that overcomes anything? It's Yours. Help me have childlike faith, not trusting in myself, but trusting in You.

AUGUST 21

*Then Jesus left the Jordan, full of the
Holy Spirit, and was led by the Spirit in
the wilderness for forty days to be tempted
by the devil. He ate nothing during those days,
and when they were over, he was hungry.*

Holy Spirit, You led Jesus when He was on earth, and You lead me, too. Sometimes I forget You are always with me. I get so caught up in my schedule that I don't remember how You promise to guide me wherever I am or whatever I do. When I am with my friends, You guide me. When I am frustrated by my family, You guide me. When I am doing schoolwork or at practice or at church, You guide me the whole time. When I forget You are with me, will You remind me? Thank You for guiding Jesus, and thank You for guiding me!

AUGUST 22

PSALM 119:90

Your faithfulness is for all generations; you established the earth, and it stands firm.

Father God, Your Word contains so many true stories that remind me why I should trust You. When I am faced with a hard situation, I sometimes struggle to trust You are doing what's best for me. I forget You are the God who shows His faithfulness throughout the whole Bible. You were faithful to provide a child to Abram and Sarah when they were too old; You were faithful to help Moses address Pharaoh when he was terrified to speak in public; and You will be faithful to walk with me through everything You call me to. Help me turn to Your Word when my faith wobbles. Thank You for giving me examples from the Bible so that I can have hope for the future.

AUGUST 23

PROVERBS 3:13–14

Happy is a man who finds wisdom and who acquires understanding, for she is more profitable than silver, and her revenue is better than gold.

Lord, Your Word says asking for wisdom is the wisest thing I can do. I typically try and determine what is right all by myself. I am good at convincing myself that I know what's best for me. I forget to come to You and ask for Your wisdom. So, God, I am asking You now: Will You give me wisdom beyond my years? Will You remind me that You hold all knowledge, and You promise to guide me in that knowledge if I just ask? Thank You for Your wisdom, and thank You for giving that wisdom to me!

AUGUST 24

2 CORINTHIANS 5:21

He made the one who did not know sin to be sin for us, so that in him we might become the righteousness of God.

Jesus, my identity is only found in You! When You died on the cross for my sins, You gave me Your identity. God doesn't see my sin when He looks at me; He sees You! The world tells me I'm defined by all kinds of things other than You: my appearance, my sexuality, my mental health, my political party, my friend group. But none of those things last. They aren't steady like You are. Will You help me put my identity only in You and reject the temptation to put my hope in anything else? Thank You for defining my life by Your love!

AUGUST 25

1 JOHN 4:16

*And we have come to know and to believe
the love that God has for us. God is love,
and the one who remains in love remains
in God, and God remains in him.*

Father God, Your love is all around me, but I don't always think it's enough. It's really hard to see everyone else around me in a dating relationship. I feel like I am constantly comparing myself to my friends, people online, or even characters in movies. So many people seem to have found "the one." Lord, will You remind me that I don't have to be dating someone to prove I am worthy of love? I am loved, because You made me, and You died and rose again for me. Any love I experience in this life is nothing compared to Your never-ending love! Help me lean into Your love. Thank You for Your love. It is enough for me.

AUGUST 26

COLOSSIANS 3:14

Above all, put on love,
which is the perfect bond of unity.

Lord, true unity only comes through You. I am so tempted to conform to people's expectations so I will be accepted. I want to be like my friends. Then they'll approve of me. In my mind, if I look and act like everyone else, maybe we will have something in common. But that's not unity. That's *sameness*. Even if I were to fit in with my friends perfectly, my relationships with other people only last when they are rooted in Your love. Will You unify me with other Christians through Your love? I don't want to conform to anything that doesn't look like You. Thank You for joining me together with other believers so that we can better reflect Your love!

AUGUST 27

MATTHEW 5:4

*"Blessed are those who mourn,
for they will be comforted."*

Father in heaven, only You bring true comfort. But all too often, I rely on myself. I think that if I can just encourage myself, I'll stop being sad about changing schools and having to make new friends. If I can just find the right mantra, I will be able to pull myself out of my depression. Will You help me push against those ideas? Bring me the peace that only comes from You. Give me a heart that relies on You as my comforter when I am tempted to rely on myself. Thank You for always welcoming me when I am sad and for loving and encouraging me when I mourn.

AUGUST 28

AMOS 5:24

But let justice flow like water,
and righteousness, like an unfailing stream.

Lord God, I want to help make things right for people experiencing injustice. It seems like the older I get, the more I learn about terrible things that happen in this world. I have always known this world is broken, but it seems like I see new, heartbreaking realities every day. I don't know exactly how, but I want to be a part of the change that only You can bring. Will You help me stand up for what's right? Will You give me the courage to speak out for justice and to join You in Your work of bringing justice to the world? Thank You for being a God who sees and cares about what's wrong in the world. I can't wait for the day when You make all things right.

AUGUST 29

JAMES 1:14

But each person is tempted when he is drawn away and enticed by his own evil desire.

God, You help me resist my sinful desires. I know my heart is evil, but I sometimes have a hard time believing it. In my mind, evil is the villain in my favorite movie or the dictator we learned about in history class. But Your Word says evil lurks in my heart, too. Without Your grace, my sin deserves the same punishment as anyone else's. Will You help me resist the temptation to rebel against You? I need Your guidance and power to say "no" to the sin that lives in my heart. Thank You for Your help! Thank You for guiding me away from evil and toward You.

AUGUST 30

MATTHEW 14:30

But when he [Peter] saw the strength of the wind, he was afraid, and beginning to sink he cried out, "Lord, save me!"

Lord, I know You want me to keep my eyes on You when things are hard. But when things are falling apart around me, I focus on my fear. I sink in anxiety, like Peter sinking in the water. I forget to trust You and in my fear, I lose sight of You. Jesus, help me focus on You when things are going well and when it feels like I am drowning in hardship. I want to spend my time praying to You and thanking You for all the good You have given me, instead of obsessing over what went wrong or what could go wrong. I am so thankful that I can always fix my eyes on You, no matter what is going on around me.

AUGUST 31

JOHN 1:3

*All things were created through him,
and apart from him not one thing was
created that has been created.*

Jesus, I can see You in Your creation. But sometimes I don't know where You are. I want to feel like I am on fire for You all the time, but I don't. I go through my day, and it seems like You aren't with me. But Lord, Your Word says You were present when the world was created. You are still holding all of creation together today. Help me remember that when You feel far away. Your creation is a promise: You have always been here. You still *are* here, and You always will be. Please draw me close to You through the things You've made. This world is so beautiful! But it's nothing in comparison to You, Jesus.

NEW

SEPTEMBER 1

2 JOHN 6

This is love: that we walk according to his commands. This is the command as you have heard it from the beginning: that you walk in love.

God, You don't always tell me exactly what I should do next, but You do tell me to walk in love. Sometimes I think following You would be easier if I just had a list of rules for every situation. How should I love a friend who abandons me? What do I do when I'm going through a painful breakup? I spend time wondering how I should follow You if the answer isn't written in the Bible. But even when I don't know what to do, I know my life should be characterized by love. Help me do what is right by loving You through every decision I make and every situation I face. Thank You for calling me to a life of love.

SEPTEMBER 2

MARK 2:5

Seeing their faith, Jesus told the paralytic,
"Son, your sins are forgiven."

Jesus, thank You for being willing and able to save me from sin. Sometimes I feel like the paralyzed man in this passage. I know the dirtiest things about myself. My thoughts remind me how sinful my heart is. If people knew what goes on in my head, would they even want to be around me? You are the only one who knows my deepest thoughts, and You still choose to cleanse me from my sin. I am so grateful for Your mercy! Please help me overcome my most horrible thoughts and trust You for forgiveness every time I sin.

SEPTEMBER 3

MATTHEW 22:37

*He said to him, "Love the Lord your God
with all your heart, with all your soul,
and with all your mind."*

Lord, I want to love You with my whole self: heart, soul, and mind. It's easy to believe going to church on Sunday or posting a Bible verse on Instagram every now and then is how I show my love for You. But I want my love for You to be so much more than that. I want to love You with my heart by making You the center of my attention. I want to love You with all my soul by trusting You completely. And I want to love You with my mind by studying Your Word, because the more I know You, the more I love You. Give me a love for You that seeps into every corner of my life. Thank You for being a God of love. Help me love You with my everything!

SEPTEMBER 4

PSALM 147:4–5

*He counts the number of the stars; he gives
names to all of them. Our Lord is great,
vast in power; his understanding is infinite.*

Father in heaven, Your knowledge blows me away. When I learn about the universe, I feel so small. You created planets and moons and galaxies. You know every star by name and every comet that races through the sky. I think about time and space, and I wonder: *How could You care about someone so insignificant as me?* But You set Your sight on me. You say people aren't insignificant. We are even more valuable than the galaxies. Thank You that with all Your knowledge and wisdom, You still choose to love me.

SEPTEMBER 5

ROMANS 12:16–18

Live in harmony with one another. Do not be proud; instead, associate with the humble. Do not be wise in your own estimation. Do not repay anyone evil for evil . . . If possible, as far as it depends on you, live at peace with everyone.

God, You call me to live at peace with everyone around me—even difficult people. When someone is mean to me, my first thought is that I should be mean back. It's easy to gossip about people who gossip about me, to fight with people who pick fights with me, or to make fun of people who make fun of me. It's hard to respond to any of those things with kindness or love. Will You teach me how to live at peace with people when I am surrounded by conflict? Thank You for teaching me to be a peacemaker through the instructions in Your Word and the guidance of the Holy Spirit.

SEPTEMBER 6

PSALM 42:5

*Why, my soul, are you so dejected? Why are
you in such turmoil? Put your hope in God,
for I will still praise him, my Savior and my God.*

Father God, I can still praise You even when I'm depressed. When I'm having my saddest day, my first instinct isn't worship. It's anger. I want to be angry with You, to blame You for my sadness. But in my heart, I know You aren't to blame. Even on my darkest days, help me praise You. Even when I am angry and feel like there is no hope, remind me how good You are. Give me hope so I can trust You, even when my heart is heavy. Thank You for being with me whether I am joyful or depressed. You never change, You hear my cries, and You are always worthy of praise.

SEPTEMBER 7

PROVERBS 3:5–6

Trust in the LORD with all your heart, and do not rely on your own understanding; in all your ways know him, and he will make your paths straight.

Lord, Your Word tells me to stop leaning on my own understanding. I usually think I know what's best for my life: what friendships to pursue, what classes to take, when to go to church and when to skip. I need Your help to make my path straight. Please always lead me in *Your* best direction instead of *my* best direction. In every moment, help me trust in You. You are a good God. You know better than I do and see further than I do. You are trustworthy, Lord, and I can always trust and follow You.

SEPTEMBER 8

PSALM 121:8

*The LORD will protect your coming
and going both now and forever.*

King Jesus, because You are with me, I never go anywhere alone. That's such good news! From moving away from home after high school to death itself—I am terrified of facing scary things by myself. I know that ultimately everything will be okay. After this life is over, I'll live in heaven with You. It's what comes *before* eternity that scares me. When I feel alone and afraid, remind me that You're with me. Even when I face my greatest fear on earth, comfort me with Your presence. You'll never leave me. You are with me everywhere I go, no matter where You call me, no matter what You call me to do, and no matter what fears I face along the way.

SEPTEMBER 9

PSALM 139:4

Before a word is on my tongue,
you know all about it, LORD.

God, You know everything I am going to say before I say it. Most of the time, I don't think about what I'm going to say before I speak. But You do. I want Your wisdom when I am getting ready to speak. If I am going to encourage someone, give me the wisdom to know exactly what they need to hear. Help me hold my tongue when I am about to criticize. And if I am tempted to gossip, remind me to stop talking before I even begin. Help me discern what words to speak before they come out of my mouth. Thank You for guiding me to honor You with all my words!

SEPTEMBER 10

JOHN 15:15

"I do not call you servants anymore, because a servant doesn't know what his master is doing. I have called you friends, because I have made known to you everything I have heard from my Father."

Jesus, thank You for being my friend. Sometimes I treat our friendship as if it only exists when I am at church or Bible study. I think about You and pray to You when I'm reminded to, but I forget about Your friendship when I am at school, with my friends, or watching TV. Will You help me live as if I am Your friend in every part of my life? I want my relationship with You to extend beyond church and Bible studies, coloring every part of my day. Thank You for pursuing a relationship with me by dying for my sins. I am so thankful I get to enjoy Your friendship forever.

SEPTEMBER 11

HEBREWS 12:14

*Pursue peace with everyone, and holiness—
without it no one will see the Lord.*

God, I want to pursue peace and holiness so I look more like You. Sometimes I wonder what people see when they look at me. Do they see pride? Insecurity? Do I seek out drama? When people look at me, I want them to see You. Please help me look more like You every day. Give me opportunities to share Your good news with people as I pursue peace and holiness instead of pride and drama. Thank You that even though I am a sinner, I can reflect a little bit of Your character to everyone around me.

SEPTEMBER 12

JOHN 8:29

"The one who sent me is with me. He has not left me alone, because I always do what pleases him."

Father, I need Your help to obey You. Without Your help, I struggle to do anything You have asked me to. I care more about what my friends think of me than what You think of me. I'd rather have people see me as cool than religious. But when I read the Bible, I see how Jesus lived on earth. He cared about pleasing You, not the people around Him. Will You help me look more like Jesus? Thank You for promising to be with me as I obey You, and thank You for giving me grace as I try to obey You.

SEPTEMBER 13

ROMANS 6:12–13

Therefore do not let sin reign in your mortal body, so that you obey its desires. And do not offer any parts of it to sin as weapons for unrighteousness. But as those who are alive from the dead, offer yourselves to God, and all the parts of yourselves to God as weapons for righteousness.

Lord, thank You for giving me a body I can use to honor You. It seems like the world tells me my body exists to serve *me*. TV shows and Instagram ads say the best thing I can do for my body is to give it whatever it wants: to have sex with whoever I want, to eat as much or as little as I want, or to show off to impress others. But sometimes, doing what I want means disobeying You. Help me love You enough that I say "no" to my desires when they go against Your will. I want to trust You to meet all my wants and needs. I am so grateful You gave me this body. Help me use it to follow and worship You.

SEPTEMBER 14

Daniel 3:17

If the God we serve exists, then he can rescue us from the furnace of blazing fire, and he can rescue us from the power of you, the king.

Father God, thank You for the story of Shadrach, Meshach, and Abednego! It's amazing. There is no threat to me that You aren't in control of. You protected them from the fire, but before You did that, You gave them faith. They knew, whether You saved them physically or not, You were in control of the situation. Even if they burned in the fire, You would be with them. Will You give me faith like that? Help me believe You are in control of even the scariest situations in my life. Whether or not I go through fires, I want to believe You are with me.

SEPTEMBER 15

PHILIPPIANS 1:6

*I am sure of this, that he who started
a good work in you will carry it on to
completion until the day of Christ Jesus.*

Lord, thank You for doing a good work in me. I sometimes wonder how You could make anything good of someone like me. After I get angry with someone or say something I regret, I see sin in my heart that I didn't even realize was there. I wonder how You—a perfect God—could possibly use someone who just said awful, hurtful things. But You do! I'm so thankful that Your goodness is bigger than my sinfulness. Thank You for showing me my sin, helping me repent, and making me look more like You.

SEPTEMBER 16

ISAIAH 1:17

*Learn to do what is good. Pursue justice.
Correct the oppressor. Defend the rights of
the fatherless. Plead the widow's cause.*

God, Your Word tells me to help others. It's easy to think of my faith as something in my head. If I *know* enough Bible verses or *think* You're trustworthy in the hardest circumstances, I can prove I have a genuine relationship with You. But Your Word says my faith in You should change the way I live. Help me fight against oppression and use my voice to stand with those who can't speak for themselves. In my weakness, You helped me. You set me free from sin and adopted me as Your child. Help me live out my faith by doing good for others.

SEPTEMBER 17

EPHESIANS 2:8–9

*For you are saved by grace through faith,
and this is not from yourselves; it is God's gift—
not from works, so that no one can boast.*

Father in heaven, sometimes I think I have to work to earn Your grace. I think if I dress modestly enough or don't say cuss words or only watch the cleanest things on TV, I'll become someone who deserves You. But Your Word tells me I can't do anything to make myself worthy of Your love. Even if I *look* like the best Christian, sin lurks deep in my heart, separating me from You. Help me to believe my salvation is by faith in Your grace alone, not by works. I can't make enough good choices to earn Your grace; I can make good choices because You've given me Your grace.

SEPTEMBER 18

1 THESSALONIANS 1:4

*For we know, brothers and sisters
loved by God, that he has chosen you.*

God, You chose me because You love me. Sometimes I'm afraid You'll take away Your love. When I lie to my parents or gossip about a friend, I feel like I let You down. How could You still love me when I knowingly sin? But Your Word reminds me how You chose me to be Your child—not because of anything I did or do, but because of Your love. I am secure in You. You know me, including all my sins, and You still made me Yours. Thank You for choosing me, God! Give me confidence in Your love. You will never take it away from me.

SEPTEMBER 19

PROVERBS 29:11

A fool gives full vent to his anger,
but a wise person holds it in check.

Lord, it's so hard to make good decisions when I'm angry. When things don't go my way, I'm tempted to go off on a friend, sibling, or my mom or dad. I want someone else to be as upset as I am. I know it's wrong, God, but sometimes I can't help it. I need Your help. Stop me from pouring out hurtful words or actions when I'm mad. I need Your wisdom when I feel out of control. Only You can help me hold back my anger and respond the way You would respond. Thank You for helping me restrain my anger. I can't do it on my own.

SEPTEMBER 20

ZECHARIAH 8:16

These are the things you must do:
Speak truth to one another.

God, I want friends who will lead me in speaking truth. Millions of people claim to have all of life's answers. I can easily find influencers who will tell me exactly how I should think, and I can always find someone who will tell me what I want to hear. They'll tell me it's okay to hold a grudge if someone hurts me or to have sex if I'm really in love. But I don't need people who will tell me what I want to hear—I need people who will tell the truth. Give me friends who love You so much that they encourage me with the truth found in Your Word. Thank You for using other people to make me more like You!

SEPTEMBER 21

GALATIANS 5:25

*If we live by the Spirit, let us also
keep in step with the Spirit.*

Holy Spirit, when I walk with You, I am more content. On my own, I want things that aren't from You. I convince myself I can watch whatever I want if it makes me happy, I can gossip about whoever I want if it makes me popular, and I can treat my body however I want if it makes me feel good. But when I walk away from what I want and start walking with You, the other things start to feel less important. When I want things that aren't from You, remind me that You are the only one who will satisfy my heart. Guide me to keep in step with You.

SEPTEMBER 22

PSALM 139:16

Your eyes saw me when I was formless; all my days were written in your book and planned before a single one of them began.

God, before anyone else knew me, You had a plan for my life. Sometimes I am so obsessed with my plans that I forget You know everything about my future. I think I know exactly what kind of school I want to go to or what kind of job I want to do or when I want to be married or have kids. Help me let go of my expectations for the future. I want to trust that You have good things in store for me—even if they don't look the way I imagined. I am so excited to see what You have planned for me. Thank You for caring about my future before I was even born!

SEPTEMBER 23

ISAIAH 40:8

*"The grass withers, the flowers fade,
but the word of our God remains forever."*

Father, when I am anxious, I sometimes struggle to remember Your promises. I go to friends for advice or look up what an "expert" has to say about my fears. But even when that advice is good, it always leaves me dissatisfied. Your Word, though, is different! Your Word lasts forever. When I focus on what You say in Your Word, I trust You more. As I study Your Word right now, let Your truths sink into my mind so I can remember them when I need them. Thank You for teaching and comforting me through the Bible!

SEPTEMBER 24

PSALM 51:6

Surely you desire integrity in the inner self,
and you teach me wisdom deep within.

Lord, You call me to a life of integrity—a life of honesty from the inside out. I can convince people I don't struggle with some of my most secret sins. As long as I don't talk about them, I can hide them. But You don't care about the way I look to others. You care about my heart. Will You help me be honest about my sin with You, myself, and other people? I want to be a person of integrity who shares my struggles and victories with sin so others can see You working in me.

SEPTEMBER 25

PHILIPPIANS 3:13–14

Brothers and sisters, I do not consider myself to have taken hold of it. But one thing I do: Forgetting what is behind and reaching forward to what is ahead, I pursue as my goal the prize promised by God's heavenly call in Christ Jesus.

King Jesus, thank You for reminding me that there is no such thing as a perfect Christian. Sometimes I read the Bible and think that people like Paul, David, and John must have gotten everything right all the time. I feel ashamed because of my sin and wonder if You could ever do anything good through someone like me. But in this passage, Paul says even he wasn't perfect! Will You help me remember You can still use me even though I am a sinner? Thank You for forgiving my sin and helping me follow You.

SEPTEMBER 26

LUKE 10:41–42

The Lord answered her, "Martha, Martha, you are worried and upset about many things, but one thing is necessary. Mary has made the right choice, and it will not be taken away from her."

Lord, thank You for being so gentle with me when I'm worried. Sometimes I feel like Martha—I get upset when everything isn't going exactly how I want. When I feel out of control and out of sorts, I stop focusing on You. I start focusing on everything I can control: my grades, my sports, or my social media presence. Instead of getting angry or yelling when Martha took her focus off of You, You were gentle. You calmed her worry and asked her to slow down and pay attention to You. Thank You for being gentle with Martha, and thank You for being gentle with me. In my worry, remind me what's necessary: slowing down and putting my focus on You.

SEPTEMBER 27

DEUTERONOMY 31:6

"Be strong and courageous; don't be terrified or afraid of them. For the LORD your God is the one who will go with you; he will not leave you or abandon you."

Lord, You know me better than anyone else on earth—even more than I know myself! I spend a lot of time being afraid of myself. I am afraid I'll make a choice that will ruin everything. Maybe I'll choose a bad friendship, a bad relationship, or the wrong path for my life. Maybe I'll sin and hurt myself or someone else. But You know my heart. You know me. You can direct my choices and help me to be brave instead of afraid. I want You to do that, God! You know when I am likely to choose sin, so will You help me follow You no matter what choice is in front of me? Thank You for knowing me and loving me so deeply.

SEPTEMBER 28

1 Peter 3:3–4

Don't let your beauty consist of outward things like elaborate hairstyles and wearing gold jewelry or fine clothes, but rather what is inside the heart—the imperishable quality of a gentle and quiet spirit, which is of great worth in God's sight.

God, I want to focus more on the state of my heart than on what other people think of me. Instagram, TikTok, Snapchat, and all the dating apps all have filters I can apply to make me look however I want. I can look stronger or skinnier. I can create flawless skin. I can edit videos that only show the best parts of me. When Peter wrote these words, people were doing the same thing: obsessing over their appearance. Will You recenter me on what matters? Give me a heart that doesn't care about showing off for others. Instead, help me to please You.

NEW

SEPTEMBER 29

MATTHEW 24:7–8

"For nation will rise up against nation, and kingdom against kingdom. There will be famines and earthquakes in various places. All these events are the beginning of labor pains."

Father in heaven, You are faithful in every situation. Sometimes when I learn about history or things happening around the world, I'm afraid. I can't imagine experiencing something like war, famine, or a natural disaster, but I know all those things are parts of this broken world. Will You help me trust You even if I experience those things? In every terrible situation, point me to one truth: this world is not my home. Thank You for promising that one day You will put an end to the brokenness of this world. You will make everything right. I can't wait to live in a perfect eternity with You!

SEPTEMBER 30

ACTS 2:44–45

*Now all the believers were together
and held all things in common. They sold
their possessions and property and distributed
the proceeds to all, as any had need.*

Jesus, I want to be as close with other Christians as the early Christians were! Sometimes I feel disconnected from other Christians. It's easier to identify with my friends who go to the same school, play the same sports, or live in my neighborhood. But You tell me that the best thing I can have in common with someone is You! Help me first to identify as Your follower. Give me a bond with other believers—they're my brothers and sisters in You. Thank You for putting other Christians in my life!

OCTOBER 1

ISAIAH 55:12

You will indeed go out with joy and be peacefully guided; the mountains and the hills will break into singing before you, and all the trees of the field will clap their hands.

God, thank You for guiding me everywhere I go. I feel You guiding me when I spend time with You in Your Word or praying, but I sometimes feel like You are far away when I'm going through my daily life. Your Word, though, tells me You aren't only with me when I'm at home reading my Bible or in church on Sunday. You are with me when I go to school on a hard day. You walk with me when I am frustrated with sports. You are right by my side when I am with my friends! Thank You for guiding me, and for always being with me, no matter where I am or what I am doing.

OCTOBER 2

HEBREWS 4:11

Let us, then, make every effort to enter that rest, so that no one will fall into the same pattern of disobedience.

Lord, it takes a lot of effort to rest in You. It feels like a thousand voices speak to me at all times. Social media influencers tell me what I "need" to buy. Instagram tells me how I should look. TikTok pressures me to go viral. When I listen to those voices, I start disobeying You. I get obsessed with stuff, appearances, or popularity. Help me quiet the voices so I can focus on You. I know it will take work, but I also know that spending time with You helps me be more obedient. Thank You that when the voices around me create chaos, You give me peace and rest.

OCTOBER 3

1 SAMUEL 1:16

*I've been praying from the depth of
my anguish and resentment.*

Father in heaven, thank You for inviting me to come to You when I am grieving. When Hannah prayed in 1 Samuel, she wasn't trying to put on a happy face. She told You and everyone around her that her heart hurt. She asked You for what she desperately wanted. Sometimes I forget I can come to You like that. I think I have to pretend I am at peace with everything in my life—even when that's the furthest thing from the truth. But You invite me to come to You in my grief, just like You did for Hannah. Help me be completely honest with You about my sadness! Thank You for being a safe place for me when my heart hurts.

OCTOBER 4

PSALM 37:23

*A person's steps are established by the LORD,
and he takes pleasure in his way.*

Lord, I want to enjoy obeying You! Sometimes it feels like a million rules come with being a Christian. When I read the Bible, I feel trapped—all I see are things I *shouldn't* do. My mind and Satan tempt me to think I won't be happy if I follow You. But God, the Bible reminds me pleasure and joy are found by walking in Your ways. Help me remember that following You isn't about following the rules. It's about loving You so much that I enjoy obeying You. Thank You for the joy that comes from chasing after You!

OCTOBER 5

JOHN 8:36

*"So if the Son sets you free,
you really will be free."*

Jesus, You bring freedom from sin! My sin nature tries to convince me everything is better than You. It says I'll miss out on something important if I go to church instead of hanging out with my friends. It tells me reading Your Word is lame. It says that if I drink, I'll be accepted by my friends. Or, if I don't have sex, I am missing out. Sometimes my sin nature says lying will get me where I want to go. Over and over again, sin distracts me from You. It lures me toward things that can never fulfill me. You are the only one who can free me from sin's attractions! Remind me that You are where real freedom is. Nothing is better than You. Thank You for dying and rising again to set me free from sin.

OCTOBER 6

PSALM 112:7

*He will not fear bad news;
his heart is confident, trusting in the LORD.*

Father God, thank You for being trustworthy, even when I receive bad news. Sometimes it feels like I'm constantly waiting for something terrible to happen. I'm scared of getting a call that someone in my family has died or that my best friend is moving away. I know at some point, bad news has to come. But Your Word says I don't have to be afraid. It says I can confidently trust You. Will You take away my fear of bad news? Give me confidence that even if something terrible happens, You can be trusted, because You are good!

OCTOBER 7

JAMES 5:16

*Therefore, confess your sins to one another
and pray for one another, so that you
may be healed. The prayer of a righteous
person is very powerful in its effect.*

Lord, thank You for giving me other Christians to confess my sins to! Your Word tells me that sharing my sin struggles with believers leads to healing. But Jesus, confessing my sin often feels embarrassing. I think I must be the only one who has terrible sin in my heart. Sometimes when I share my struggles with other people, I'm not completely honest. I tell them the things that are easier to say, like the little lies I tell my parents or how I was mean to a sibling or cousin. I think that if I hide the darkest things, people will think better of me. Will You give me the confidence to confess the sin I am most ashamed of? I don't want to be alone in my struggles; I want to be healed of them.

OCTOBER 8

PSALM 127:2

*In vain you get up early and stay up late,
working hard to have enough food—yes,
he gives sleep to the one he loves.*

God, my hard work means nothing without You. If I am not intentional about spending time with You and praying throughout my day, I start to trust myself. I get through my busy schedule. I believe the best part about me is what I can accomplish: if *I* am a good student or the most talented person in the room, my day was worthwhile. But Your Word says that without You, every "A" I get, every game I win, and every bit of talent I share is all in vain. It doesn't mean anything without You. Help me to rely on You every day, and give me the wisdom to know when I need to stop, rest, and focus on You.

OCTOBER 9

1 CORINTHIANS 7:35

*I am saying this for your own benefit,
not to put a restraint on you, but to promote
what is proper and so that you may be
devoted to the Lord without distraction.*

Jesus, I could spend hours and hours scrolling through my phone or watching funny videos. I would spend all day messaging my friends if I could. But when I stop and think about how much time I spend on those things versus how much time I spend with You, the Holy Spirit convicts me. He nudges me to give up distractions so I can focus on You. I want to be rooted in You, not my phone, Jesus. Will You help me put away anything that distracts me? I want to devote more time to my relationship with You. Thank You for always being ready to spend time with me, and for giving me a desire to spend more time with You!

OCTOBER 10

ECCLESIASTES 4:10

*For if either falls, his companion can
lift him up; but pity the one who
falls without another to lift him up.*

Lord, thank You for putting people in my life who lift me up when I fall. When I start to sin, I'm afraid to tell anyone. What if I get judged? I hate feeling alone, but sometimes it seems like I am following You all by myself. Will You give me friendships with people who want to lift me up? Give me people I can walk with so when I stumble into sin, they're there to help me. Put people in my life who won't think less of me, but who will love me and challenge me to keep following You. Thank You that I don't have to follow You alone.

NEW

OCTOBER 11

ACTS 20:32

*And now I commit you to God and to
the word of his grace, which is able to
build you up and to give you an
inheritance among all who are sanctified.*

God, Your grace saves me and helps me become more like Jesus! Before I believed in You, I had no desire to be like You. I was totally satisfied with just being myself: following my own heart and doing the things I wanted to do, without ever once thinking about You. But since You saved me, You are forming me into a person who is more and more like Your Son. I feel convicted when I sin, and I find myself wanting to spend time reading the Bible or praying or talking about You with my friends. Will You keep changing my heart? Thank You for giving me grace I don't deserve!

OCTOBER 12

LUKE 8:14

"As for the seed that fell among thorns, these are the ones who, when they have heard, go on their way and are choked with worries, riches, and pleasures of life, and produce no mature fruit."

Lord, help me love You more than I love anything else in the world. I sometimes worry I will become obsessed with success when I am an adult. It would be easy to spend my life trying to get the next promotion or only thinking about how I can make more money so I can have the nicest house or the nicest clothes. I don't want any of those things if that means not following You. Will You keep my heart focused on You now so I can resist the temptation to chase money and success in the future? I need Your help. Grow in me a love for You that surpasses my love for anything else.

OCTOBER 13

PROVERBS 9:13–15

Folly is a rowdy woman; she is gullible and knows nothing. She sits by the doorway of her house, on a seat at the highest point of the city, calling to those who pass by.

Father God, I don't want to live a life that's all about me. Most of the time, when I am trying to make something all about myself, it's because I'm insanely focused on myself. I'm proud and loud rather than humble and wise. I show off because I want other people to know how good I am. When I'm tempted to show off or call for people to pay attention to me, remind me that my focus should be on You. Thank You for calling me out on my pride and for helping me center my attention on You.

OCTOBER 14

EPHESIANS 4:15

*But speaking the truth in love, let us grow
in every way into him who is the head—Christ.*

Jesus, Your Word tells me that truth and love go hand in hand. It's really hard to do both of those things at the same time. I tend to speak to people with either one or the other. I don't tell people the truth because I don't want to hurt their feelings. Or I tell them hurtful things that are true, but leave love out of the equation. Help me speak truth *in* love when I talk with others. I want to be gentle and kind as I tell the truth *because* I love them. I know it won't be easy, but that's exactly how You speak to me, Lord. You are always honest, and You are always loving. Thank You that with Your help, my words can sound a little more like Yours.

OCTOBER 15

PSALM 62:5

Rest in God alone, my soul,
for my hope comes from him.

God, my hope only comes from You. Sometimes I put my hope in other things—and they're not always bad things. I put my hope in making the right grades. I want to impress my parents or teachers. Or I try to be the best athlete or the most talented artist so crowds will cheer for me. But no matter how impressive I am, I am always left wanting to hear one more "good job." Will You help me put away my need to impress people? Putting my hope in You is the only sure thing. Only You can satisfy my heart and give me rest.

OCTOBER 16

EPHESIANS 2:10

For we are his workmanship,
created in Christ Jesus for good works,
which God prepared ahead of time for us to do.

Lord Jesus, You created me to be in this place and in this time, and You have a specific purpose for my life. You placed me in my specific family, in my exact school, and in this moment in history. And You didn't make a mistake! I want to do good works for You in all those places. Help me reflect You as I obey my parents and honor my family. Help me share the gospel when I'm at school, and give me the opportunity to point others to You every day. Thank You for making me with creativity and purpose.

OCTOBER 17

MARK 2:27

*Then he told them, "The Sabbath was made
for man and not man for the Sabbath."*

Father in heaven, help me take rest more seriously.
I need to schedule time in my week to spend with
You, and only You. Sometimes I think the Sabbath
was just an Old Testament thing—it doesn't apply
anymore. How could I possibly take a whole day—
twenty-four hours—to rest?! But even in the New
Testament, You asked people to set aside a whole
day of the week to spend time with You. I usually
feel too busy to rest in You, but when I don't, I miss
out on the opportunity to grow my relationship with
You. Will You remind me to spend time with You regularly, God? Thank You for the gift of rest!

OCTOBER 18

PSALM 138:8

*The LORD will fulfill his purpose for me.
LORD, your faithful love endures forever;
do not abandon the work of your hands.*

King Jesus, You have beautiful plans for broken people. Sometimes I feel like I am letting everyone down. When I can't keep up with my school work or when I don't do well in sports or music, I feel like I'm not enough. What if I never am? And, if I can't be who people need me to be, how can I possibly be what You want me to be? Thank You for reminding me that You are bigger than my brokenness. You will fulfill Your plan in my life even though I am weak. Thank You for never abandoning me, even when I let You down!

OCTOBER 19

*Love one another deeply as brothers and sisters.
Take the lead in honoring one another.*

God, I sometimes get caught up in chasing perfect friendships. I want people around me to be positive and kind and never hurt my feelings. When someone hurts me, it's easier to walk away and find a new friend. Will You make me care more about *being* a good friend than *finding* good friends? I want my love for other people to outweigh my expectations that they'll be perfect. Encourage me to be quick to serve and to honor the friends You've given me. Thank You for the gift of friendship! I want to be the best friend I can be, like You are for me.

OCTOBER 20

LUKE 19:40

He answered, "I tell you, if they were to keep silent, the stones would cry out."

Dear God, creation points us to worship You, whether we do or not. When I am keeping up with school work, after-school activities, and friends, I sometimes get overwhelmed and forget to worship You. Even when the things I am doing are good and necessary, I need to make praising You my top priority. Will You give me an attitude of constant praise? Help me worship You as the Creator! You made everything, and Your creation gives little clues about who You are and what You are like. Thank You for leading me to worship even when my heart forgets. I love You, Lord.

OCTOBER 21

LUKE 12:25

*"Can any of you add one moment to
his life span by worrying?"*

Holy Spirit, worry isn't from You. It doesn't help
me at all, so why do I still do it? I worry about big
things and little things—from getting my work done
when school gets busy to people abandoning me,
and from getting embarrassed at school to what
the future of the world will be. It's so easy to tailspin
into anxiety. I need You to interrupt my worry-filled
thoughts! When I worry, will You remind me You
are faithful? Help me remember that even if all my
worries come true, You are still good. Thank You for
helping me with my worry.

OCTOBER 22

Do not be hasty to speak, and do not be impulsive to make a speech before God. God is in heaven and you are on earth, so let your words be few.

Father, when I don't like what You have planned for me, I sometimes talk back to You. I question whether You *really* know what's best for my life. Even though I say I trust You, my heart likes to trust itself. It's easy to worship You when I like what's happening in my life. It's a lot harder when it seems like nothing is going my way. Thank You for reminding me that You know so much more than I do. You are in heaven and see all that is happening on earth! When I am tempted to question You or talk back to You, remind me of Your knowledge and wisdom. I am so thankful that You know so much more than I do!

OCTOBER 23

MATTHEW 26:42

Again, a second time, he went away and prayed, "My Father, if this cannot pass unless I drink it, your will be done."

Jesus, when You prayed to God before You died, You asked for what You wanted and for God's will to be done. I don't know how to do those two things at the same time. When I really want something like better grades or to get on the varsity team or even to date someone, it's hard to accept Your answer if You say "no." Most of the time, I would rather have my will than Yours. Help me love You the same, no matter how You answer my prayers. Will You give me the confidence to ask for what I want *and* the faith that You are good, no matter what Your answer is? Thank You for showing me how to pray and how to trust You in every circumstance.

OCTOBER 24

1 JOHN 3:19–20

This is how we will know that we belong to the truth and will reassure our hearts before him whenever our hearts condemn us; for God is greater than our hearts, and he knows all things.

Father in heaven, the ugly accusations that come from my heart aren't from You. Sometimes I feel ashamed. I remember some of the worst things I have done—the lies I have told, the times I have cheated, the ways I have deceived people so I could get my way. When I focus on what I've done wrong in the past, I can start to wonder if You've really forgiven me. Thank You that You have! You know my worst sins, and You forgive me. When I remember my past, help me to stop feeling ashamed and start celebrating how good You are instead.

OCTOBER 25

MATTHEW 28:20

*"And remember, I am with you always,
to the end of the age."*

Jesus, sometimes I feel alone when I am telling other people about You. I wish You were right there with me, especially when people ask me questions I don't know the answers to. But before You went back to heaven, You told Your disciples to share the gospel everywhere they went. You told them that even though You weren't with them physically, the Holy Spirit would be. Help me remember You're always with me when I share You with others, and even when I don't know what to say. Thank You for always being with me. You never leave my side.

OCTOBER 26

JOHN 17:17

*"Sanctify them by the truth;
your word is truth."*

Dear God, thank You that I can trust the Bible! I experience a lot of peer pressure. It sometimes seems like everyone is doing something I know I shouldn't do, whether it's online, in school, or in my group of friends. I know that without Your help, I will give in to temptation. But here's what else I know: Your Word helps me say "no" to peer pressure and "yes" to good instead. Help me turn to Your Scriptures so I can be encouraged to do the right thing. Thank You that when I open the Bible, I can be sure that everything I read is good, true, and inspired by You!

OCTOBER 27

GALATIANS 6:2

*Carry one another's burdens; in this way
you will fulfill the law of Christ.*

Lord, Your Word tells me to carry other Christians' burdens. Sometimes when I'm with other believers, we have a hard time sharing our struggles with one another. I think we are afraid we might be judged for our weaknesses or for not obeying You. No one wants to look like a bad Christian or someone who needs help. Lord, I want to become someone other people come to when they are burdened by sin. Help me encourage them with my words and actions. Give me wisdom to help people turn away from sin and look toward You. Thank You for carrying my burdens; help me carry other people's burdens, too.

OCTOBER 28

JAMES 3:5–6

So too, though the tongue is a small part of the body, it boasts great things. Consider how a small fire sets ablaze a large forest. And the tongue is a fire. The tongue, a world of unrighteousness, is placed among our members. It stains the whole body, sets the course of life on fire, and is itself set on fire by hell.

God, I want my words to be helpful, not hurtful. The Bible says words can be so destructive they're like a forest fire. The fire burns hot, grows quickly, and is almost impossible to put out. I have been hurt by other peoples' words. When I remember what they said about the way I look or the clothes I wear, or something worse, my heart hurts. Will You make me someone who does the opposite? I want to stop hurtful words from leaving my mouth. Thank You for warning me about the power of words. Help me honor You with everything I say!

OCTOBER 29

JONAH 2:1

*Jonah prayed to the LORD his God
from the belly of the fish.*

God, sometimes I act like Jonah. I completely disobey You even though I know better. I lie when I know how much You value truth; I disobey my parents instead of honoring them; I give in to all kinds of temptations. I choose my way instead of Yours. When You told Jonah to go to Nineveh, and he went the opposite way, You called him back to You with the big fish. He prayed to You, and You heard him—even after his reckless disobedience! Help me be like Jonah in the fish. I want to come humbly to You in prayer after I have disobeyed You. Thank You that even after I sin, You invite me to repent and come back to You.

OCTOBER 30

PSALM 34:18

The LORD is near the brokenhearted;
he saves those crushed in spirit.

Father, when my heart is broken, You come close to me. I am afraid of experiencing a huge tragedy—the loss of a loved one, a terrible disease, my friends abandoning me. Your Word tells me that when my heart breaks, You come near in a special way. Help me focus on Your goodness as You draw near to me. Heal my heart whenever tragedy strikes. Give me peace in Your promise that You are with me and You see me in my pain.

OCTOBER 31

*But you, LORD, are a shield around me,
my glory, and the one who lifts up my head.*

God, You protect me better than any person ever could. When I'm afraid, I trust my parents or an adult to keep me safe. When I get in trouble, I know someone will be there to help me. While You have provided people to protect me from harm, You are the only one who can protect me from sin and its consequences. I want to trust You more than any person I know—more than my parents, more than my pastor, more than my teachers, and more than my siblings or friends. Thank You for being the one who is ultimately protecting me! Give me more faith in You than in any other person.

NOVEMBER 1

ROMANS 8:1

Therefore, there is now no condemnation for those in Christ Jesus.

Jesus, because of Your death and resurrection, I am not condemned! You don't hold my sin against me. But sometimes all I hear are Satan's accusations: *God's forgiveness isn't for a liar like you. How could God really love a friend who is as bad as you? God saw that sin, and now He's going to stop loving you.* But the promise in Your Word is louder than Satan's harshest accusation. There is *no* condemnation, not now, not ever! You took all my guilt and shame away, and I don't have to listen to Satan's lies anymore. Thank You for forgiving me of my sin completely and for never holding my past against me.

NOVEMBER 2

MICAH 6:8

Mankind, he has told each of you what is good and what it is the LORD requires of you: to act justly, to love faithfulness, and to walk humbly with your God.

Lord, when I see bad things in the world, they overwhelm me. How could someone like me do anything about oppression against vulnerable people or disease or poverty? I think, *I don't have time or someone else will do it or I'm not old enough to make a difference.* But Your Word says I should act justly, love faithfulness, and walk humbly at all times, not when it's convenient for me or when I feel I'm strong enough. Thank You for being the most just, faithful, and humble person to ever exist and for giving me the power to be those things, too!

YEAR

NOVEMBER 3

PHILIPPIANS 2:9–10

For this reason God highly exalted him and
gave him the name that is above every name,
so that at the name of Jesus every knee will bow—
in heaven and on earth and under the earth.

King Jesus, You are the only one worthy of worship! In my mind, worship is singing songs in church or praying. It's hard to know when my heart is worshiping something other than You. But when I care more about scrolling Instagram than reading Your Word, I worship Instagram. If I value what my friends think of me over what You think, I'm giving my friends my worship. And when I obsess over my grades, I'm worshiping success. Please show me all the things that take my worship away from You—especially when I don't realize it's happening. I love You, Jesus. Help me praise You as the King, because You are!

NOVEMBER 4

PROVERBS 23:18

For then you will have a future,
and your hope will not be dashed.

God, no matter how scary the future looks, I can always trust in You. The older I get, the more I see how terrifying my life could be. It seems like the world is always on the brink of war. I am afraid of a worsening climate bringing more natural disasters. On a personal level, I have no idea how to be an adult and take care of myself. I might be worrying about the future right now, God, but I don't need to. You will be with me even if there are wars, tornados, earthquakes, or hurricanes. You will be there when I don't know what to do next. You will make all the terrifying things in this world right again. Thank You for giving me hope for the future!

NOVEMBER 5

GALATIANS 3:28

There is no Jew or Greek, slave or free, male and female; since you are all one in Christ Jesus.

Father, Your kingdom isn't exclusive. I shouldn't be, either, but my friends and I sometimes leave people out. We struggle to include people in our group if we can't relate to them. If a kid is new to my school, doesn't play sports, or just seems different somehow, I don't know how to connect. But when I exclude people, I miss an opportunity to learn more about You through them. I give up the chance to love someone You love. I may even give up a moment to share the gospel with a person who needs to hear it. Please help me see differences, not as reasons to separate from someone, but as opportunities to celebrate how we are united by Your love!

NOVEMBER 6

PROVERBS 10:27

The fear of the LORD prolongs life,
but the years of the wicked are cut short.

Dear God, my relationship with You should be the highest priority of my life. The world tells me to prioritize other things. It says to hurry up and get everything done now so I can make all my dreams come true. When I think I have to do another activity to fill up my college résumé or take another hard class to bring up my GPA, I don't feel like I have time to focus on my relationship with You. Will You help me make my relationship with You the most important thing? Help me fear You. I want to be so amazed by Your presence that I can't help but focus on You. When other things feel more important, I want to believe they're not! Thank You for challenging me to place my priorities where they really matter.

NOVEMBER 7

1 TIMOTHY 4:7–8

But have nothing to do with pointless and silly myths. Rather, train yourself in godliness. For the training of the body has limited benefit, but godliness is beneficial in every way, since it holds promise for the present life and also for the life to come.

God, I want to train my mind in godliness so I know when people aren't telling the truth about You. Some of my friends say I can find You through any religion. Others think that if I am just a good enough person, I can get to You. When I start listening to them, it's easy to doubt You are the only God, and the only way to You is through Your Son. Will You help me grow in godliness by reading my Bible, praying, and doing everything I can to know You more? I won't do well on a test if I don't study; I won't run faster if I don't practice; and I won't become more like You if I don't train my mind. Help me to hold fast to the truth in Your Word so I'm not swayed by the lies of the world.

NOVEMBER 8

MARK 10:27

Looking at them, Jesus said, "With man it is impossible, but not with God, because all things are possible with God."

Lord, nothing is impossible for You! When I read about miracles in the Bible, they seem like science fiction. I haven't seen a miraculous healing or a person walk on water with my own eyes—I've only seen those things in movies, TV shows, or books set in a fantasy world. But when You were walking on earth, You did things that are impossible for people. You made blind people see. You made people who had never walked a day in their lives able to run. Will You help me believe in Your miraculous power even if I am not seeing it in my everyday life? Help me trust that even if I can't wrap my mind around it, all things are possible for You!

NOVEMBER 9

COLOSSIANS 1:13–14

He has rescued us from the domain
of darkness and transferred us into
the kingdom of the Son he loves. In him we
have redemption, the forgiveness of sins.

Jesus, Your Word says You rescued me from darkness, forgave me of my sin, and redeemed me. I can see You now! I have hope that will last forever! But so many of my friends and family members don't know You. They're still walking in the darkness. All I want for them is to be in Your light. Thank You for forgiving me, for helping me leave my darkness and walk in Your light. Please rescue my friends and family, too. Help them to see how much better Your light is than darkness so they can experience the joy of Your forgiveness. Thank You for Your rescue plan! Please rescue the people I love!

NOVEMBER 10

*For the LORD your God is the one
who goes with you to fight for you against
your enemies to give you victory.*

Father, the Bible says You fight my biggest battles for me. It's easy to think my battles are with my friends when we get mad at each other or with my parents when they aren't letting me do something I want to do. But the truth is, my battles aren't with other people. They're with my own sinful desires. Sometimes I want so bad to be popular that I'm willing to hurt other people to get it. I want to date someone, so I lie to my parents about where I'm going. Help me remember I am not fighting alone. You are with me as I battle my sinful heart. Thank You for joining my fight and giving me victory I could never achieve on my own!

NOVEMBER 11

ECCLESIASTES 5:15

As he came from his mother's womb, so he will go again, naked as he came; he will take nothing for his efforts that he can carry in his hands.

Lord, there is nothing I will gain on this earth that I'll take with me when I leave. It's so easy to become obsessed with what I can gain: the best clothes to show off what I can afford, the most followers so everyone will want to be around me, a video that goes viral because I'm so funny. But I won't take name-brand shoes or Instagram followers or a video with a million likes with me when I die. None of that will matter. It'll all disappear. But some things won't disappear: my relationships with people, a godly character, and Your Word. I don't want to spend my life chasing things that don't last; I want to care more about what is eternal.

NOVEMBER 12

MARK 16:15

*Then he said to them, "Go into all the world
and preach the gospel to all creation."*

God, I want to live out my faith with words! I know
I should talk about You, but I often choose not to.
It's easier to stay quiet so I don't upset anyone or
come across as pushy about what I believe. I feel
the Holy Spirit nudging me to share the gospel, but
I ignore that nudge. Will You help me talk about You
even when it might feel uncomfortable? Give me so
much love for You and Your truth that I can't help
but bring You into my conversations. Thank You for
using me in Your plans to share the gospel with people around me!

NOVEMBER 13

GALATIANS 6:4

Let each person examine his own work,
and then he can take pride in himself alone,
and not compare himself with someone else.

Lord Jesus, I trust You are doing a good work in me, so why do I constantly compare myself to others? When I am reading my Bible every day or praying more often than my Christian friends, I think of myself as a "better" Christian. I become proud, and I think I must be more spiritually mature than everyone else my age. But it turns out—I am the one being immature. I think I'm focusing on You, but really, I'm making my faith all about me and how great I am. Will You humble me? Make me someone who works hard for You, because I love You, without making myself the main character of the story.

NOVEMBER 14

ROMANS 12:2

Do not be conformed to this age, but be transformed by the renewing of your mind, so that you may discern what is the good, pleasing, and perfect will of God.

Father God, when my friends are living in sin, it makes me want to sin, too. I am afraid of what people will think of me if I follow You. But Your Word reminds me that You want me to follow You unapologetically, no matter what the rest of the world thinks. I get to have You by my side 100 percent of the time! Help me remember that You are with me so I have the courage to leave a huddle of gossip, turn something inappropriate off the TV, or change my language to sound more like You. Thank You for walking with me as I follow You.

NOVEMBER 15

1 THESSALONIANS 5:21

Test all things.
Hold on to what is good.

Jesus, people tell me different ways to read and understand the Bible. Some people say You literally created the world in six days, and others say it's metaphorical. Some Christians say it doesn't matter how much I go to church—my relationship with You is personal. Some people even tell me I have to do certain works to be saved. Sometimes, their bad teaching is obvious. Other times . . . I don't know what to believe. I need Your help. Please guide me in testing what people say about You. When I read the Bible, help me understand what it says. I want to hold on to good teaching and reject anything that's not true.

NOVEMBER 16

MATTHEW 5:6

"Blessed are those who hunger and thirst for righteousness, for they will be filled."

Lord, help me crave a right relationship with You! Most days, I am more addicted to my screen than spending time with You. Whether it's binge-watching a show, scrolling through hours of TikToks, or creating a post that will get a ton of likes and reactions, I never feel like I have done enough online. I always want more. Will You take away my addiction to likes and follows? Give me a hunger for a right relationship with You instead. You are the only one who satisfies. When I spend time with You, I am never left discontent or dissatisfied. Thank You for being everything I need.

NOVEMBER 17

ISAIAH 14:24

As I have purposed, so it will be;
as I have planned it, so it will happen.

God, no one can derail Your plan! In a world of pandemics, wars, and immoral leaders, I sometimes wonder where You are. How could You possibly have a plan in a moment of history that has so much death and destruction? Can You really make anything good out of evil? Thank You for Your reminders. Even in history's most horrible moments, You are in control. Give me faith in You when it seems like all the good in the world is gone. Thank You that there is no disease or dictator more powerful than Your plan!

NOVEMBER 18

1 JOHN 5:14–15

This is the confidence we have before him: If we ask anything according to his will, he hears us. And if we know that he hears whatever we ask, we know that we have what we have asked of him.

Father in heaven, give me confidence when I pray to You. Sometimes I feel like I shouldn't ask You for what I want. I am afraid if You tell me "no," I'll feel let down and lose trust in You. It's such a relief to know You want me to come to You with what's on my heart. You want me to tell You if I am afraid of something or want something, and to trust that You will hear my prayer. I know my prayers won't always be perfect—I'll ask for the wrong things or with bad motives—but You ask me to pray to You anyway. Please give me a heart that comes to You always and wants Your will above everything else.

NOVEMBER 19

PSALM 16:11

You reveal the path of life to me;
in your presence is abundant joy;
at your right hand are eternal pleasures.

Lord, I sometimes believe if I do spiritual things, like reading my Bible or worshiping at church, then You will be with me. But Your Word says You can be with me in every area of my life! Will You remind me of that? Help me remember You're with me when I am with my friends, when I'm doing my homework, when I am at lunch, and even when I am deciding what TV show to watch or what music to listen to in my free time. I want to experience the abundant joy of Your presence in the spiritual parts of my life *and* the normal parts of my life. Thank You for the joy and pleasure of Your presence!

NOVEMBER 20

PHILIPPIANS 4:6–7

Don't worry about anything, but in everything, through prayer and petition with thanksgiving, present your requests to God. And the peace of God, which surpasses all understanding, will guard your hearts and minds in Christ Jesus.

Jesus, the Bible says I shouldn't worry about *anything*. But that feels impossible. I am worried about my next big test, what happens if I lose a parent, and even the world's future. How am I supposed to stop worrying when wars, diseases, and death are everywhere? How can I stay calm when it feels like my whole future rests on my GPA? One little test could completely derail everything! I need Your help. I can't stop worrying, but I can respond to my worry with prayer. When anxiety creeps into my heart, help me pray instead of giving in to worry. Thank You for Your promise. You give me peace in the middle of my anxiety, and it makes no sense to me. But that's because it only comes from You!

NOVEMBER 21

ISAIAH 40:29

*He gives strength to the faint
and strengthens the powerless.*

Father, You are the only one who strengthens me when I am exhausted. It feels like my life is filled to the brim. Between school and friends, sports and arts, church and family, I get overwhelmed by all the things I have to do. I'm tired. I think if I can just drink more caffeine or get one extra hour of sleep, I'll have the energy I need. But God, there is no quick fix. Help me rely on You to lift me up when I feel weary and powerless. Thank You that You are the one who gives me strength to be faithful in every part of my life.

NOVEMBER 22

MATTHEW 12:34

*"For the mouth speaks from
the overflow of the heart."*

Lord God, my words are an overflow of my heart. Sometimes I can't believe the things I say. I'm embarrassed at how I talk, but I know the words coming out of my mouth are evidence of what is going on inside me. When I gossip, help me see I'm not loving people the way You tell me to. When I talk back to my parents, show me how my heart dishonors them. If I lie to someone, reveal how I'm not valuing truth. Thank You for giving me a peek into my heart through the words that come out of my mouth. Please shape my heart to look more like Yours. Then my words will start to change and honor You!

NOVEMBER 23

GALATIANS 2:20

I have been crucified with Christ, and I no longer live, but Christ lives in me. The life I now live in the body, I live by faith in the Son of God, who loved me and gave himself for me.

God in heaven, thank You that I am no longer defined by my sin! Sometimes I wonder if all You see when You look at me is what I do wrong. I wonder if You still see the person I was before I believed in You. Or maybe You look at the worst parts of me now. I feel so guilty, ashamed, and afraid. I don't want to come near You because You might see the *real* me—the sinner. When I am spiraling in shame, remind me of the truth: You don't see my sin, You see Your Son! When You look at me, You see His sacrifice. Thank You that You don't identify me by my sin, but as Your child.

NEW

NOVEMBER 24

PROVERBS 2:6–7

*For the LORD gives wisdom; from his mouth
come knowledge and understanding. He
stores up success for the upright; He is
a shield for those who live with integrity.*

Father, all wisdom and knowledge is from You! It's easy for me to buy into the world's message that being smart is the most important thing. I am so thankful for the opportunity to learn more—I believe You can use my teachers and school to teach me—but sometimes when I feel really smart, I get prideful. I think if I can just learn more, I will be able to have all the knowledge and wisdom I need to be successful. I need a different heart. Will You give me a heart that relies more on You than on my own mind? When I get prideful, help me to recognize You as the wisest and most knowledgeable being to exist.

NOVEMBER 25

PROVERBS 19:20

*Listen to counsel and receive instruction
so that you may be wise later in life.*

Lord, thank You for giving me a community of believers who help me grow in wisdom. I'm embarrassed to share my struggles with other Christians. They seem so much better at following You than me! I don't feel like anyone is as sinful as I am, and I don't want them to think less of me. Please remind me that You want me to be vulnerable with other believers! You placed them in my life so they can share their wisdom—Your wisdom. Help me to ask my biggest questions and to share my greatest struggles with Your followers. Thank You for speaking to me through my Christian community.

NOVEMBER 26

PSALM 145:13

*Your kingdom is an everlasting kingdom;
your rule is for all generations. The LORD is faithful
in all his words and gracious in all his actions.*

God, You are the ultimate promise-keeper! I put a lot of trust in the adults in my life. I trust that my parents will protect me, that my teachers will help me, and that my church leaders will encourage me. But sometimes even the adults I trust most let me down. I'm so thankful You placed people in my life who I can trust, but I know there is no one—not my parents, not my teachers, not my church leaders—who I can trust like I trust You. Thank You for always keeping all Your promises. Help me place my faith completely in You!

NOVEMBER 27

ISAIAH 66:13

As a mother comforts her son, so I will comfort you, and you will be comforted in Jerusalem.

Lord, thank You for being my comforter. When my life feels the most uncomfortable—I am entangled in conflict with friends, stressed out about school, or overwhelmed by all my commitments—I need You! The Bible tells me Your comfort is even better than a mother consoling her baby. Your comfort is gentle, it's kind, and it's sure. Remind me of those truths when my life is far from comfortable. Thank You that I can count on You to be my peace and to be my help no matter what circumstances I face.

NEW

NOVEMBER 28

MATTHEW 26:41

*"Stay awake and pray, so that you
won't enter into temptation.
The spirit is willing, but the flesh is weak."*

Holy Spirit, I need Your help resisting temptation. When my life feels easy, and when I am not actively being tempted to sin, I forget to pray. I forget it's in those exact moments that I should prepare for hardship and temptation. In the garden of Gethsemane, Jesus told the disciples to pray so they wouldn't enter temptation, because He knew what was coming. So did You. You knew the disciples would be asked if they knew Jesus. Please remind me to pray before temptation comes so I am ready to say "no" to sin and "yes" to You. I am so grateful that You use prayer to make me more like Jesus.

NOVEMBER 29

PSALM 51:10

*God, create a clean heart for me and
renew a steadfast spirit within me.*

Father, please keep renewing my heart to love You more. I am so thankful that You forgave me of my sin once and for all when I believed in Your Son. But my heart is still sinful. I hold grudges toward people. I think lustful thoughts. I roll my eyes at the way You want me to live. Even though You forgave me, I need help making my heart more like Yours. Please continue to change me. Help me forgive people as You forgave me. Cleanse my mind of ugly thoughts. Help me love Your Word way more than anything else. I will need Your help cleaning my heart for the rest of my time on earth. Thank You for promising to help me do that.

NOVEMBER 30

ROMANS 8:38–39

For I am persuaded that neither death nor life, nor angels nor rulers, nor things present nor things to come, nor powers, nor height nor depth, nor any other created thing will be able to separate us from the love of God that is in Christ Jesus our Lord.

God, I am so thankful that nothing can ever separate me from You! Sometimes, my friends and family tell me that trusting in You is foolish. If I am being honest, I sometimes believe them. I start to doubt Your goodness. But You tell me that nothing—not even my own doubts and fears—can separate me from Your love. You are not mad at me. You gently call me back into Your presence. Father, please help me remember You are holding me tight. I cannot be pulled away from Your presence by anything at all.

DECEMBER 1

PSALM 36:7

How priceless your faithful love is, God!
People take refuge in the shadow of your wings.

God, Your love is worth more than anything on earth! Sometimes when I'm at school, I get jealous of my friends' stuff. I see kids with crazy-nice clothes. It seems like everyone has the latest technology, and there are even some kids who have huge social media followings. When I can't keep up with everyone else, I feel angry. I stop focusing on how much You've given me and start obsessing over everything I don't have. Will You help me remember that there is no possession worth more than Your love? When jealousy sinks into my heart, please point me back to You!

DECEMBER 2

*And be kind and compassionate to
one another, forgiving one another,
just as God also forgave you in Christ.*

Dear God, Your grace overwhelms me! Sometimes I forget how much You've forgiven me, and I don't forgive friends and family when I feel hurt. I convince myself that what they did to me is worse than anything I've ever done. But that's not true, Lord. Please remind me of Your love when it's time for me to extend love, too. Make me someone who is quick to give grace because I remember the grace I've been given. I know that I am just as much in need of Your forgiveness as anyone else. Thank You for being gentle with me when I sin. Show me how to do the same for my friends.

DECEMBER 3

JOHN 5:19

Jesus replied, "Truly I tell you, the Son is not able to do anything on his own, but only what he sees the Father doing. For whatever the Father does, the Son likewise does these things."

Jesus, thank You for giving me an example of how to follow Your Father's will! On my own, there's no way I can follow You like I want to. I want to be liked, even if it means going to parties or getting into a relationship that doesn't honor You. I am constantly tempted to show off in front of my friends just to look cool or feel more popular. When You fought temptation, You looked to the Father. When I fight temptation, help me look to You. I want to follow Your example, but I need Your strength. Help me to stop caring about what others think of me. Thank You for being the greatest example of loving, faithful obedience that I could ask for!

DECEMBER 4

EPHESIANS 1:11

*In him we have also received an inheritance,
because we were predestined according to the
plan of the one who works out everything in
agreement with the purpose of his will.*

God, thank You that Your plan for me is better than anything I could come up with on my own! The Bible says I have received an inheritance. You count me as one of Your children. So why do I struggle to trust that Your plans are best? I am really afraid that my future won't work out the way I want it to. What if I don't get into my favorite school? What if I never date anyone? What if I can't get the job I really want one day? I can't see my future, but I want to be someone who trusts You in all things. Thank You for working out Your plan for my life!

DECEMBER 5

1 JOHN 3:2

Dear friends, we are God's children now, and what we will be has not yet been revealed. We know that when he appears, we will be like him because we will see him as he is.

Lord, the Bible tells me that one day, my body will be made completely new and it will be perfect! It's easy to obsess over the world's standards of the "perfect" body. The world tells me that perfection has a specific weight, a particular skin tone, or a certain eye color or hair texture. Please help me to stop believing in the world's definition of beauty! I want to embrace the body You have given me and to look forward to the day when You give me an eternal body like Yours. I don't know what that body will look like, but I do know that not even the most "perfect" body on earth can compare.

DECEMBER 6

PROVERBS 9:8

Don't rebuke a mocker, or he will hate you;
rebuke the wise, and he will love you.

Father, help me respond to people's correction with wisdom. When someone tells me I am wrong, I would rather make excuses than admit fault. If my teacher tells me I need to try harder on an assignment, I tell him all the reasons I didn't have time. When my parents ask me to do better with my chores, I get defensive and disrespectful. Even when the Holy Spirit convicts me of sin, I justify why I haven't repented yet. Help me see correction as helpful. It is something that helps me honor You in every part of my life. Thank You for giving me people who want me to be a more faithful follower of You!

DECEMBER 7

ROMANS 14:19

So then, let us pursue what promotes peace and what builds up one another.

Lord, I want to live a life of peace and encouragement! It's so easy to see others as competition. I am always fighting to be the best: to have the most impressive grades, to be the first chair, to start the game, or even to look like the most faithful Christian. I want people to see all my hard work and recognize me for my accomplishments. But You created people to live in peace with one another, not in competition. Please make me a better encourager than a competitor. Help me take my eyes off myself and build others up instead. Thank You for giving me a peace that only comes from You and guiding me to make peace with others.

DECEMBER 8

HEBREWS 4:16

Therefore, let us approach the throne of grace with boldness, so that we may receive mercy and find grace to help us in time of need.

Lord Jesus, thank You that I can pray with boldness when I sin! Lord, I sin every day. Sometimes it feels insignificant, like lying to my teacher. Other times it feels unforgivable—like having sex outside of marriage. When I feel like I have messed up too much for Your forgiveness, please remind me that I don't have to shrink away from You. I can come to You with confidence! You will forgive me and help me repent and turn away from any sin. As long as I live on this earth, I know I'll fight temptation. Sometimes I will even give in to that temptation. I can't pull myself out of sin on my own. But in Your mercy, You give me help I don't deserve. Thank You, Jesus.

DECEMBER 9

PSALM 55:2

Pay attention to me and answer me. I am restless and in turmoil with my complaint.

Father, You are the only one who gives peace in my uncertainty. I desperately want to control all the unknowns in my life. I want to know what I'm going to do after high school. I want to know if the person I'm dating will break up with me. I want to know if my friends are talking about me behind my back. But God, no matter what circumstance I face, You already know. You are holding me as I face the unknown. Please give me peace as I wait for answers to all my questions. Remind me that You will be with me every step of the way.

DECEMBER 10

MARK 6:31

*He said to them, "Come away by yourselves
to a remote place and rest for a while."
For many people were coming and going,
and they did not even have time to eat.*

Father, it's not just spiritual rest You want me to prioritize; You ask me to pursue physical rest, too. I have so many things I am responsible for and so little time to do them. Sometimes I feel like I have to stay up all night doing homework to prove that I'm a good student. Or I put in extra hours of sports practice to make sure I'm the best. In those moments, I stop prioritizing what my body needs. But You don't want me to run myself into exhaustion. You want me to trust You, to believe that even if I don't get everything done, You will still be with me. It's so comforting that You genuinely care about my body. Please help me to choose rest so I can care for my body the way You do.

DECEMBER 11

ECCLESIASTES 3:13

*It is also the gift of God whenever
anyone eats, drinks, and enjoys all his efforts.*

God in heaven, thank You for the gift of joy! I don't usually think about the little things I enjoy as gifts from You, but I should. I want to see moments of happiness as opportunities to worship. I can worship You when I am laughing with my friends, when my mom makes my favorite meal, when I see a really good movie, and when I breathe a sigh of relief after earning an "A." Thank You that this whole world isn't full of only death and destruction. Even in a sinful place, Your gifts remain, and I can delight in them. I'm so glad I get to experience these little joys in my life. Help me see them as evidence of Your kindness.

DECEMBER 12

ROMANS 12:15

*Rejoice with those who rejoice;
weep with those who weep.*

Lord, You ask me to empathize with people who are hurting. Sometimes I don't try to understand other people's pain. If I have never experienced something, I can't wrap my mind around the pain they feel. Trying to understand what they're going through isn't very comfortable. It's easier to stop the conversation by telling them a Bible verse or giving them advice on how to feel better. But when I am hurting, I don't always want advice. I just want someone to sit with me, be sad with me, and love me even if they don't understand what I am feeling. Please make me someone who can do that for others.

DECEMBER 13

1 KINGS 19:12

*After the earthquake there was a fire,
but the LORD was not in the fire. And after
the fire there was a voice, a soft whisper.*

Father, Your guidance isn't always found in the loudest voices. When I need to hear from You, I want You to shout from the rooftops, to tell me exactly what to do! I want a miraculous sign: to hear Your voice audibly, to turn to the exact passage in the Bible, or to be told by my pastor on a Sunday morning what I need to know. And while You may show up in a loud voice, You sometimes appear more quietly. I need Your help listening for You in the stillness. I want to hear Your voice in the pages of Your Word when I'm least expecting it, when I am praying in silence, or even as I am driving to school, thinking about my day. Thank You that whether You come with a thundering voice or in the stillness of the morning, You are speaking to me.

DECEMBER 14

1 CORINTHIANS 13:11

When I was a child, I spoke like a child, I thought like a child, I reasoned like a child. When I became a man, I put aside childish things.

Holy Spirit, please help me to grow into a mature Christian. Sometimes I wonder if I am really growing all that much. I make decisions I'm not proud of. I struggle to read my Bible because I get sucked into social media. Sometimes I stop praying because I doubt You're listening. I need Your help growing spiritually. On my own, I make childish decisions, but with You, I can grow to look a little more like Jesus. Thank You for being with me as I grow. Please make me someone who recognizes when I am acting childishly and looks to You for growth and guidance.

DECEMBER 15

ACTS 1:14

They all were continually united in prayer, along with the women, including Mary the mother of Jesus, and his brothers.

Jesus, sometimes I think of prayer as something I should do on my own. I forget You want me to pray *with* other people. It connects us! When there is drama in my friend group, remind us that we can ask You to guide us. When I am not getting along with my parents, help us go to You as a family. If another Christian hurts my feelings, give me the confidence to ask if we can pray together before I act in anger. Thank You that even when I feel upset or frustrated with other believers, You use prayer to unite us!

DECEMBER 16

1 CORINTHIANS 15:33

Do not be deceived:
"Bad company corrupts good morals."

Lord, please help me know when and how to leave bad friendships. I don't want to leave friends who need Your love. But when I am around certain people, I'm more tempted to sin. I see them sneaking behind their parents' backs to go to parties or have sex, and I believe those things must not be that big of a deal. I don't want to be swayed to sin, but I want to be a light to my friends who aren't following You. Please help me walk away from friendships that keep me from following You in a way that shows my friends Your love *and* honors You. I know I can't do that on my own. Thank You for promising to help me.

DECEMBER 17

PSALM 23:2–3

He lets me lie down in green pastures;
he leads me beside quiet waters.
He renews my life; he leads me along
the right paths for his name's sake.

Father God, help me enjoy the time I spend resting in You. When I slow down to spend time with You, I feel like I'm missing out on something. I might miss my favorite influencer's Instagram story or an invitation to hang out with my friends or even time to study for a test. A thousand things try to take my attention from You at any given moment. Please remind me that when I spend intentional time with You—not doing anything else—it's the best thing I could be doing. You renew my spirit! Thank You for leading me to spend time with You and to rest in Your presence without fear of missing out on anything else. I want to desire spending time with You, because You are good, and You love me.

DECEMBER 18

The integrity of the upright guides them, but the perversity of the treacherous destroys them.

God of heaven, thank You for the reminder that dishonesty brings destruction. I sometimes believe little lies aren't big deals. I tell my parents my grades are better than they are; tell my friends that someone flirted with me just so I will look cool; and even lie about my faith if I think I'll get judged for following You. But I don't want to lose anyone's trust. I don't want to misrepresent You by making myself into a liar. Please give me integrity. Help me to be honest with everyone, even if it means disappointing my parents or not looking cool for my friends. Thank You for convicting me when I am tempted to lie!

DECEMBER 19

DEUTERONOMY 8:3

*Man does not live on bread alone but on every
word that comes from the mouth of the LORD.*

Jesus, I need Your Word as much as I need anything else! I don't understand parts of the Bible right now. Should the laws in the Old Testament mean anything to me? Am I supposed to understand ancient languages? Shouldn't I just wait until I am smarter or older to read Your Word? I might not understand everything, God, but I know You want me to love the Bible. I can't learn to love it if I don't read it, so please motivate me to open the pages of Your Word every day! Help me make sense of the things I don't understand, and send people who will answer my questions. Thank You for joining me as I take the journey into loving Your Word!

DECEMBER 20

TITUS 3:4–5

But when the kindness of God our Savior and his love for mankind appeared, he saved us—not by works of righteousness that we had done, but according to his mercy—through the washing of regeneration and renewal by the Holy Spirit.

Lord, no matter how hard I try, I can't save myself. Sometimes I think my good works make me worthy of Your love. I think that when I am reading my Bible every day, really paying attention in church, inviting friends to Bible study, and praying before every meal, I'm someone You can be proud of. Then I stop. I stop reading the Bible because I get busy; I get distracted by my phone in church; or I miss an opportunity to share the gospel because I'm embarrassed by my faith. Please remind me it's only because of Your love that I am accepted and chosen. Thank You for loving me before I ever opened the Bible or prayed for the first time. Help me remember that it's Your love that saves me—not my works.

DECEMBER 21

2 CORINTHIANS 4:16

Therefore we do not give up. Even though our outer person is being destroyed, our inner person is being renewed day by day.

God, thank You that when I feel weak, You renew me! I never think I measure up to people around me. Someone will always be more athletic, smarter, or better looking than I am. When I put my hope in those things, I feel let down every time I don't measure up. But when I'm not completely focused on the outside, You renew my heart. You're always renewing my heart, even when I *am* caught up in comparing myself to others. Would You remind me that You care about what's on the inside of me? Please help me to stop comparing myself to others. Make me more concerned about the way I represent You to the world. Thank You that when I can only see my weakness, You renew me in Your strength.

NEW

DECEMBER 22

2 PETER 3:9

The Lord does not delay his promise,
as some understand delay, but is patient
with you, not wanting any to perish
but all to come to repentance.

Lord Jesus, I want to be patient with other people when I share the gospel, but sometimes I get discouraged. When I tell others about Your love and they don't believe me, I feel like they're rejecting me. I get embarrassed that I said anything in the first place. I wonder if there is any hope that they'll become Christians. I need You to remind me: You were patient with me. You waited for me to repent and never gave up on me. You were gentle with me and didn't once dismiss me as too much of a sinner. Please help me believe You are doing the same for others. Thank You for not giving up on sinners like us!

DECEMBER 23

1 PETER 4:8

Above all, maintain constant love for one another, since love covers a multitude of sins.

Father, help my love for other people reflect Your love for me! You sacrificed everything for me—You gave up Your throne to come to earth to love and serve people. But for me, it's not easy to give up anything to love others. If I want to be popular, I leave people out. If I want to have free time, I avoid serving my family. Please help me care more about loving others than anything else. Help me befriend the new kid. Make me excited to give up my free time to help my siblings with their homework or my parents around the house. Show me opportunities to set aside my own comfort so I can serve someone else. I want to be self-sacrificing for the sake of love, just like You.

DECEMBER 24

GENESIS 3:15

I will put hostility between you and the woman, and between your offspring and her offspring. He will strike your head, and you will strike his heel.

Father God, ever since sin entered the world, You planned to send Jesus! When Adam and Eve sinned in the garden, You could have just walked away from them. But instead, You created a plan to save people just like them—people like me. I choose to sin, too, God. I lie to my parents and gossip behind my friends' backs. I laugh at jokes that don't honor You. Sometimes I pretend not to be Your follower when I'm embarrassed by You. You brought redemption by sending Jesus into human history. Thank You for redeeming me. Even though I sin, I can trust in Jesus. He saves me from the consequences of disobedience. Help me to focus on the gift You gave sinful people like me: Jesus.

DECEMBER 25

LUKE 2:11, 14

*Today in the city of David a Savior was
born for you, who is the Messiah, the Lord. . . .
Glory to God in the highest heaven,
and peace on earth to people he favors!*

Jesus, You are the Savior of the whole world!
Sometimes I forget that when I go online. I start comparing myself to others. I see peoples' new gifts, pictures of boyfriends and girlfriends, and friends whose family lives look better than mine. But I don't want this day to be about comparing myself to others. Today, I get to celebrate the night You entered time and space. You left Your throne, humbling Yourself, and came into the world as a vulnerable baby. I want to worship You. When I get distracted by comparison, help me turn back to You, the Savior!

NEW

DECEMBER 26

PSALM 94:19

When I am filled with cares,
your comfort brings me joy.

God, when I am spinning with anxiety, You are the ultimate comforter. I feel a lot of pressure from my friends, even when they don't mean to pressure me. When I look at their designer clothes, their boyfriends and girlfriends, even their willingness to go to parties with the more popular kids, I feel like I need to keep up. There is almost nothing that makes me more anxious than feeling behind or left out. But You remind me that when I feel like I am going to explode from all the pressure, I can run to You. When the pressure to keep up with my friends brings distress, Your comfort brings me joy.

DECEMBER 27

1 CORINTHIANS 10:13

No temptation has come upon you except what is common to humanity. But God is faithful; he will not allow you to be tempted beyond what you are able, but with the temptation he will also provide the way out so that you may be able to bear it.

Lord, thank You for providing a way out of temptation. Sometimes it feels like I am drowning in sin. Surely no one will understand why I can't shake the temptation to lie or cheat on a big test or join in the gossip. When I feel like I am too weak to say "no," will You remind me that no temptation to sin is stronger than You? You can and will help me say "no" to any temptation I face. Help me remember that even when I can't find my way out of sin's grip, You will guide me. Help me trust in You to lead me out of temptation and into the joy of obedience.

DECEMBER 28

PSALM 14:3

All have turned away; all alike have become corrupt. There is no one who does good, not even one.

Jesus, Your Word tells me there is no such thing as a good person. But the world says we are all basically good people. As long as I have the best intentions, things will go well for me. Even though I know better, it's easy to convince myself that You love me because of my personal goodness. When I'm tempted to believe I deserve Your kindness, please humble me. Help me remember that outside of You, I can't do any good. I don't deserve Your love, but You freely give it to me. I want to spend the rest of my life worshiping You, not because of my goodness, but because of Yours!

DECEMBER 29

PSALM 19:7

The instruction of the LORD is perfect, renewing one's life; the testimony of the LORD is trustworthy, making the inexperienced wise.

Father, I get so frustrated when I don't understand the Bible. I wish You wrote a chapter directly to me. I wish You'd tell me if I should date, which schools to apply to, or how to respond when my parents are being unfair. When I feel like the Bible is missing something, that it's not telling me what I need to know, will You remind me of its perfection? You didn't leave anything out. Your Word is perfect. Please give me wisdom when I'm reading the Bible so I can uncover truths about how I should live. I am so thankful that even when I don't completely understand Your Word, I can trust it. You will reveal truth through Your Word.

DECEMBER 30

MATTHEW 6:33–34

"But seek first the kingdom of God and his righteousness, and all these things will be provided for you. Therefore don't worry about tomorrow, because tomorrow will worry about itself. Each day has enough trouble of its own."

King Jesus, when I am seeking Your kingdom, I don't have to worry about anything. But I get so caught up in temporary things. When my friends gossip about me, I think my social life is over. When I make a bad grade, I fear my GPA and future are ruined. When someone breaks up with me, I think no one will ever like me again. Every bad thing in my life feels never-ending. But they're not! The Bible says every bad thing is temporary. One day You are going to rule the earth and make it completely new. Gossip won't have a place in Your kingdom. I won't have to prove myself at school, either, and I am and will be eternally loved by You. Thank You that when I focus on Your kingdom, I stop worrying about the future.

DECEMBER 31

1 JOHN 3:1

See what great love the Father has given us that we should be called God's children—and we are! The reason the world does not know us is that it didn't know him.

Father, as I get ready to enter a new year, help other people see Your love shine through me! I want to honor You by obeying my parents—even when it feels weird. I want to make You known by sharing the gospel with my friends. I want people to ask me about Your love when they see me reading my Bible, going to church, or praying. Help me be unashamed about being Your child! Thank You for growing my relationship with You this year. Please help me overflow with love for You this next year so every person I know and love might become Your child, too.

NOTES

_____

_____

_____

_____

_____

_____

_____

_____

_____

_____

_____

_____

_____

_____